The Numbers of Your Life

Numerology and Personal Discovery

Maiya Gray-Cobb

Schiffer Publishing Ltd

4880 Lower Valley Road • Atglen, PA 19310

Acknowledgments

Grateful thanks to my wonderful, hard working editor, Dinah Roseberry, who has worked extremely hard to bring this book to perfection. My thanks also to Stacey McNutt and Chris McClure in marketing, Terri Jones, and the design team.

Schiffer Books are available at special discounts for bulk purchases for sales promotions or premiums. Special editions, including personalized covers, corporate imprints, and excerpts can be created in large quantities for special needs. For more information contact the publisher:

Published by Schiffer Publishing, Ltd.
4880 Lower Valley Road
Atglen, PA 19310
Phone: (610) 593-1777; Fax: (610) 593-2002
E-mail: Info@schifferbooks.com

For the largest selection of fine reference books on this and related subjects,
please visit our website at
www.schifferbooks.com
We are always looking for people to write books on new and related subjects.
If you have an idea for a book, please contact us at
proposals@schifferbooks.com

This book may be purchased from the publisher.
Please try your bookstore first.
You may write for a free catalog.

In Europe, Schiffer books are distributed by
Bushwood Books
6 Marksbury Ave.
Kew Gardens
Surrey TW9 4JF England
Phone: 44 (0) 20 8392 8585; Fax: 44 (0) 20 8392 9876
E-mail: info@bushwoodbooks.co.uk
Website: www.bushwoodbooks.co.uk

Library of Congress Control Number: 2012950638

Cover image Number Soup © puentes. Courtesy of www.bigstockphoto.com

Designed by Mark David Bowyer
Type set in Lucida Calligraphy / Book Antiqua

ISBN: 978-0-7643-4142-7
Printed in the United States of America

Contents

Introduction

Numbers, numbers, and more numbers. Everywhere we look we find these ciphers. We are so accustomed to them, they hardly register with us any more. But just stop and think about it for a moment. We have a social security number and a medical number to identify us. Then there is our bank account number for our money, our credit card numbers to enable us to pay later – and if we don't pay it off all at once, the balance in *numbers* causes us to pay interest – also written in numbers.

When we travel, the buses are numbered for guidance and convenience, as well as the platforms at the railway stations. The airlines, the planes – and the cockpit – have numbers; and so do the highways. We have registered car plate numbers to connect us to our insurance companies, also written in numbers on invoices. Streets, houses, apartments, hotel rooms, all have their own numbers; so do telephones and TV channels and computers. When we shop, the grocery aisles are numbered for our ease along with the names of the items we wish to buy. Clocks and thermometers are numbered, so are paints and wallpapers, even the pages of books are numbered and the spines carry the Dewey Decimal system of numbers.

Actuaries constantly work with numbers and decimals. The numbers they come up with inform insurance companies via mathematics, and the numbers they come up with define the length of your life expectancy for the insurance company to decide what kind of risk you are when you apply for life or health insurance. Now the company knows how much to charge you. Money equals numbers and vice versa. When you have an accident, an actuary will inform your lawyer and your insurance company how much your accident is worth. Again, numbers equals money and what you will get out of it.

Then we have the Elliot Wave theory, the Fibonacci numbers, the Kondratieff Cycle being used to track the future money market. Traders use them to analyze the financial market cycles, forecasting market prices (numbers) which unfold in specific patterns. These business cycles rely on investor psychology. Crowd psychology moves between optimism and pessimism in natural sequences, numbers 1, 3, and 5 are the impulses and motivations and number 2 and 4 are the correctives and restructuring. We humans are subject to the rhythms of the universe, so it is relatively easy to calculate our activities quite far into the future.

As you can see, so many things represent numbers, yet few register within our thinking patterns.

Even simple things like calendars and appointment books that we buy each year and cannot do without have numbers for each day of the week throughout the year. Months are both numbered and named. When we are born we are assigned a number for the day, month, and year of birth, along with a name which can also be broken down into numbers. In fact, all our days are numbered.

These two important personal items, given to you at birth, represent your personality derived from your name, and from your birth date comes your path in life – your destiny. This is the book that will tell you all – who you are, your in-depth psychology, and where you can take your life to *your* advantage.

Your given name has a distinctive energy/vibration pattern. When the letters are broken down into numbers and the numbers are added together, a numerologist can see your characteristics, your qualities, and your hidden traits. The letters of the alphabet represent numbers as follows. (This chart can also be found in the Appendix for easy access in later chapters.)

Letters	Equal	Number
A, J, S	=	1
B, K, T	=	2
C, L, U	=	3
D, M, V	=	4
E, N, W	=	5
F, O, X	=	6
G, P, Y	=	7
H, Q, Z	=	8
I, R	=	9

The total of the numbers of your full name somewhere between 1 and 9 indicate your personality – the impression you make on your world, how you communicate and express yourself. Some numerology books refer to this as your Expression number. Let's look at a small example of a name by assigning the name numbers from the prior chart:

C	L	A	U	D	I	A		H	O	L	M	E	S
3	3	1	3	4	9	1		8	6	3	4	5	1

24 = 4 + 2 =**6** 27= 7 + 2=**9**
Add **6** + **9** = 15 =6

Final numbers must be between 1 and 9.

The numbers for Claudia add to 24; then the 2 + 4 added together equal 6.

Holmes adds up to 27, then adding the 2 + 7 together equal 9 .

Then the whole name added together, 6 plus 9, becomes 15, then 1 + 5 becomes 6.

Claudia's whole name vibration is a 6 and she would express herself to the world as a caring, sympathetic person, enjoying marriage, motherhood, and family. She is also very much a crafts person, so it is quite likely she would work at home in some creative or artistic endeavor. This is only a very small portion of the energy pattern of Claudia Holmes. The rest of the picture will come alive when the consonants and vowels of her name are considered along with her birth date.

The **consonants** of your name indicate how you show yourself to the rest of the world – this is the mask you wear. The missing consonants point to dreams and desires you inwardly harbor.

The **vowels** contain your hidden (inner) reality; another name for this is your shadow self. The missing vowels are the underlying influence – the hidden motivations from your subconscious that influence your thought, decisions and then your actions. I have not done these for Claudia but we will get further into them in chapter 4.

Your **birth date** – year, month, and day – when added together become your **Life Path Number** pointing to *your* choice of path in life with all your strengths and weaknesses.

The missing numbers in your chart between 1 and 9 indicate the lessons you are likely to learn throughout your life and show the challenges and areas you should concentrate on. With the addition of your birth date, you will be able to see the direction your future is likely to take.

Even relationships – compatibility with others – can be judged by the mutual exchange of the energy patterns within the name numbers.

How can this be so? Everything in the universe is a vibration, and energy patterns can be seen and felt when they come together. People are simply energy patterns at birth, and the given name, when reduced to numbers, indicates how these different energy patterns come together expressing who we are.

The next chapter has the full description of the different aspects and energies of the numbers, but here briefly are a few.

- **Number 1** represents the personal self image that we all have.
- **Number 2** includes feelings and sharing.
- **Number 3** is representative of personal creativity and versatility.
- **Number 4** indicates instincts and practicality.
- **Number 5** displays change and adaptability.

- **Number 6** represents love, beauty and nurturing.
- **Number 7** shows areas of discipline and reliability in the material world.
- **Number 8** involves our money-making ability and practicality.
- **Number 9** showcases our innate talents, wisdom, and spiritual creativity.

This fascinating array can be seen in much more detail within the full chart when the different aspects and energy patterns of numbers 1-9 come together.

This numerology book will show how you can chart your own numbers with relative ease. From your birth date, you will find your path in life – your talents and strong points. With your name, you can decide if you are in the right job or relationship. You can see your weak points, parts of your personality and character that let you down at inappropriate moments, then find the balance numbers with their interpretations that will see you through the rough times. You will learn how to plot the hurdles and challenges, the cycles and rewards, the periods of growth, and the development of mind, body, and spirit. Here is where you can plumb the depths of your own psyche.

Most numerology books appear to work with numbers separately, and often fail to show the reader how to connect the numbers and energy patterns to point out the weaknesses and strengths of character and how these can be utilized to the best advantage. Chapter 5 does what other books do not. It pulls the whole chart together with a diagram showing how the numbers interact with each other.

With the permission of my student, Claudia, I shall carry excerpts of her life throughout the book as example. I shall discuss her weaknesses and negative attitude and determine where they stem from, then show the strength of the other numbers as she changes her attitude and allows her tremendous creativity to surface.

As you follow along, putting your own chart together, chapter by chapter you will dip into the depths of yourself, finding quirks, attitudes and talents you were not aware of. This quest for self knowledge through the wonderful world of numerology will open up the story of your life bringing transformations and confidence to you.

This is *your* life long journey of adventure and self discovery.

Chapter 1

Vibrations and Energy Patterns of Numbers

If you have never encountered the subjects of numerology, astrology, graphology, palmistry or biorhythms before, (all of these subjects are based on numbers), I wouldn't be surprised if you are quite skeptical about the title of this particular chapter. Read on.

As you read further into the pages of this book, you'll find yourself quite intrigued with the way numbers speak for themselves and how we humans respond to them. What we have here are the ideas and beliefs that numbers do have an impact and effect on people – that they give off a particular vibration and energy pattern to which we respond and they affect us in various ways.

This knowledge was known to Pythagorus, a Greek mystic, mathematician, and philosopher. He was called the Father of Numerological Analysis. He rediscovered the world of numbers and recognized the unity of all things in the universe – everything is just one vibration containing many aspects of itself. He understood that numbers represented the forces of the universe – that the universe itself was built on the logical flow of numbers. Number 1 being the beginning, obviously followed by number 2, then 3, then 4, each following another until 9 comes up completing a cycle.

Life within the universe and our physical plane are constant cycles. We have our recognized and expected cycles within a year – spring follows winter, summer follows spring, autumn follows summer, and winter follows autumn; then the cycle begins again. The stars in the heavens follow their own cyclical patterns: Sunspots follow an eleven-year cycle and animals have their own cycles of migration times and birthing times. We humans also have our own cyclical patterns and circadian rhythms. There are mathematical correlations between various rhythms.

Throughout our lives we continually go through cycles that influence us for certain periods of time. There are three major cycles of growth each lasting about 27/8 years. Then there are shorter cycles of 9-year lengths based on the 9 cardinal numbers whose influence you are about to learn. Finally, there are the personal cycles of years and months which you will learn to put into operation from chapter 10 onwards. These are the progressive portions of your original personality chart.

Meanwhile, it is necessary that you should absorb the separate meanings of the 9 cardinal numbers to be able to apply them to the chart that you will draw for yourself with the information in the next chapter. Do you recall when you first went to school your beginning lessons were learning the ABCs and the numbers before you learned how to write to put them all together?

Same thing here, but much more fascinating because it concerns you and the reality you are creating for yourself through your own thoughts and actions, as you react to the vibrations of the various numbers.

What is a vibration and how does it affect you?

According to my dictionary, a vibration is "a feeling or an impression that someone or something gives off." Now, think about this: If you are asked to quickly speak out a number between 1 –9, without giving it any special thought, you will immediately and subconsciously make a selection. This particular number has impressed itself on you, the vibration you respond to. This will be the one that you automatically respond to, it will be your first choice in a gambling selection, the beginning of a phone number, your post box, house or apartment number, and more than likely, will be either the addition of your name number or your birth date. You see, numbers are the energies of invisible influences to which we all respond in our own way and these are very visible in your numerology chart.

Now let's get into the numbers. It is quite likely that you will be able to recognize some portions of your character and personality as you digest the following information.

Number Meanings

Number 1

Here is the team leader, forceful, bold, active, with a great deal of executive and organizing ability. This number also stands for new beginnings whether it is a new start in life, the beginning of a new personal year cycle, a new job or career – anything that represents a new start cutting off from the old and the outworn. With this much confidence, this is the type of person who knows who he/she is, recognizes all their inner resources, knowing precisely where he/she is going.

Number 1 has a great deal of vitality, creativeness, leadership, originality, and intellectual qualities. It can also be aggressive, ambitious, and goal oriented, but often failing to plan ahead properly, being somewhat anxious to achieve whatever goals they have mind. Nevertheless, there's a great deal of self reliance and concentration. They can be relied upon and will accept heavy responsibilities and do all they can to help people who are in distress. With these qualities, there can be much achievement – even to the point of being a genius.

If there are many number 1s (A, J, or S) in the reduction of your name and very little balancing energy from other numbers, the weaker side of this number can show itself through quite powerful, arrogant, egotistical patterns. It can be the instigator of both good and evil having strong stubborn opinions of right and wrong. Intolerance, narrow-mindedness, conceit, and "putting others down" are also some of the less admirable influences of this number. Being overly independent causes dislike from others especially when advice is offered about a project and rejected in a haughty manner even though it is obviously doomed to failure. This type of number 1 should release some of the self confidence and be more open to receiving the opinions of older and more experienced people. There is too much maleness here. There is a need to consider the other numbers in the chart that can help develop warmth and a genuine feeling of sensitivity. The feminine qualities of spontaneity, tenderness, and receptivity are needed to balance the energy.

Number 2

People of this energy type are much more gentle compared to the number 1s. This energy is considered to be of the feminine type. It is an accepted fact that the odd numbers 1, 3, 5, 7, and 9, exude male energy (lively, productive, impulsive, forceful) and the even numbers 2, 4, 6, and 8 are of the female balancing type (passive, flexible, warm, and receptive) that can be very useful to the over-balanced types like the number 1 if there is an energy line between the two numbers. This can work in the opposite way – number 1 energy boosting a weak number 2 energy line. You will learn to assess the energy lines in chapter 5.

Number 2s are dualistic by nature, needing to see both sides of a question, an argument, or discussion, although they can be somewhat infuriating by "sitting on the fence," failing to making a decision. It is frequently a case of: *Should I? Perhaps not. I'll think about it. Maybe tomorrow!* Brooding and indecision are two of their prominent weaknesses.

These are people who need people; they like to be part of groups and social activities. Their tact and refinement bring many invitations; apart from that, they are the diplomatic peacemakers of this world. Somehow their strong intuition guides them into knowing just what others need and want and they are always ready to cooperate. They seem to have the innate ability to give out excellent advice, but don't ask them to make a decision for you. This unfailing judgment makes them very popular, but also causes them to take on other people's problems or responsibilities as they like to see balance in other people's lives as well as their own.

Just as number 1 is the team leader, number 2 is the team member, preferring to follow rather than lead, although they are quite capable of organizing, detailing, and handling people if absolutely necessary – but only when they have developed self-confidence and decision making.

When number 2 becomes the authority figure, this is when they discover who they really are and what they can become. Their shyness moves into the background and their inner powers start to develop. This is the most sensitive of the nine cardinal numbers, tending to be vulnerable and uncertain. Being criticized brings on upsets and hurt feelings. Number 2s just can't handle it and deliberately try to avoid it until their inborn inner strength and awareness helps to develop a strong backbone towards authority figures. When this happens they are no longer co-dependent.

Where number 1 is full of self reliance, number 2 needs to develop it. Their *major* weakness is being ultra-sensitive concerning security. They feel they cannot go it alone and must have a partner to lean on. They like to feel protected and tend to rationalize that a close relationship will bring the love and happiness they seek. If this is not forthcoming a really negative attitude can develop. Depression takes hold along with a lack of continuity in planning and self confidence takes a further dive leaning towards low self esteem. If they feel wronged in any way, they can become malicious and over critical of friends. Excessive number 2 energy (many letters B, K, and T which come under number 2, or additions totaling number 2) can cause them to become apathetic, even indifferent towards other people and to the job they are working on. This would be a pity because this number has a spiritual connection that is not found in other numbers making them the perfect power behind the throne with anything they become involved in, mainly because they deal with the world on a conscious level.

Regarding male and female energies, these are alternating positive and negative forces – or if you wish – action and non reaction. Therefore, if there are sufficient male energies – number 1s - in the chart, then this energy will give backbone and stamina to overcome the weaker portions of self. This also works in the opposite way as number 2 can give sufficient energy to number 1 to halt any impulsiveness, bringing a certain amount of balance within the number chart. When you draw up your own chart you will see that all numbers from 1-9 are represented but all at different energy levels and you will understand more clearly.

Number 3

Number 3 is the creative outcome of the blending of the energies of number 1 and 2 (1 plus 2 = 3).

Number 1, the singleton, came on the scene saying "Here I am – look at me."

Number 2's duality of feelings says, "I cooperate and share with you."

Number 3 is the triad, the triangle, the multiplicity. It is the trinity dimension recognized as the completion of body, mind, and soul energy. It is also expressed in other ways such as the trinity of the Father/Son/Holy Ghost – the three-fold godhead. Then we have the three magi with their three gifts. It is time – past, present, and future; space – length, height, depth; birth, life, and death. Everything has a beginning, a middle, and an end, and number 3 is considered as a completion, but a type of different completion to number 9 which is finality, a completion of a cycle. In the world of three, it is Being, (number 1), Consciousness (number 2), Joy (number 3) forming a triangle.

Number 3 represents creative expression. It is just one third of this complete cycle. This triangle represents the body, the creative physical expression. Numbers 4 , 5 and 6 represent another third; this triangle is the creative expression of the mind, and the numbers 7, 8, and 9. The last triangle is where we can deal with the depth of the unconscious and patterns of the soul. All these numbers communicate with each other in some way when a numbered chart is drawn up. We live in such an interactive three-dimensional world where all these numbers become part of each other. No wonder we are such complicated beings!

If you look within this 1-9 cycle, when numbers 1, 2, and 3 are added together, they equal 6. Now add together 4, 5, and 6, they total 15; and 1 + 5 = 6. Next, add 7, 8, and 9. They total 24 = 2 + 4 = 6. When these three triangles of numbers are added together, 6 + 6 + 6, they total 18. 1 + 8 = 9. Once more, we are back to the complete cycle of number 9. In fact, if you add all the numbers from 1-9, they total 45. These two numbers added together once more total 9. See how interactive these energy patterns are?

Number 3 is the triple power of spirit (number 9) and intellectual development (number 6) furthered by the conscious individual effort of number 3. Eventually, this becomes spiritual awareness directed by the energy of number 8 but developed into the shape of force, matter, and consciousness by the number 4. At another level, there is the creativity, emotions, and the material world which produce another triad of success, expansion, and recognition which is where most number 3s are, if this number dominates the number chart. At this level, 3 says ,"Let's combine the energies of the two previous numbers (1 and 2) and get on with creating something." Always the creative inner subconscious urge is anxious to produce something.

Number 3 is the outward going expression of personal and physical creativity. An excellent energy for a stage performer – dancer, singer, actor, or a person whose personal goals lend towards impressing large numbers of people, such as an artist who develops a very personal and distinctive style. It is essential for some form of communication to take place for this number whether it is speaking, writing, filmmaking, teaching, whatever appeals to them in the communicating line. A well-directed number 3 well versed in litigation can be very useful in a conflict situation where a third person is needed or called upon to decide an issue between two people.

Number 3 people are usually quite goal oriented. A well-activated number 3 has the ability to attract money, achieving success, but only if a purpose, a goal, a destination, and an outline of the achievement to be pursued is put into operation in advance. If not, disorganization and lack of focus and discipline can bring failure. These are three major negative aspects of the number 3.

The basic characteristics of 3s are usually self confidence, an easy expression of communication, along with optimism and enthusiasm. The creative talents of this number frequently encourage others to develop their own creativity, for they have the wonderful ability to inspire and motivate, whether it is students, large crowds of people, audiences, or rioters with subversive intentions. People are impressed by the outgoing, extroverted, warm personality of number 3s and would like to follow in their footsteps.

Action and initiative are a natural part of the joy of life for number 3s. Whatever they set their minds to or put their creativity and talents to work on sets them apart from other people. Number 3s are often called "lucky" and this is due to their charming, cheerful, friendly attitude, which draws people towards them, including a retinue of the opposite sex on whom they are inclined to waste their money!

If number 3 receives sufficient energy from number 4, they will have a calm nature, be sensible and ethical, good at saving and managing money. On the other hand, because they enjoy being the center of attention, they tend to show off. They love to be admired, and when this happens, it brings out their love of pleasure, encouraging them to be wasteful with their money, even getting into gambling. They can also be vain, superficial, gossipy, and irresponsible. If they are not successful or do not get the attention they think they deserve, the other side of their nature shows up. They can become moody, disorganized, cynical, and begin to scatter their energies. Becoming emotional and vulnerable, lacking focus, discipline, and direction, they are likely to have difficulty in finishing projects and their impressive creativity will go to waste.

Numbers work both ways – spiritual and material, good and not so good, positive and negative, and they need other numbers to balance and direct the energies of each other. You will note that the energies of numbers 1 and 2 joined together produce 3, and 3 creates the idea of something from this multiple energy. It can be a marriage, a baby, a book, a piece of music, a movie, anything that can be created that you care to name. This creative idea joins with the number 4 energy forming a solidity bringing it into the material world.

Number 4

If you visualize the triangular shape of the top of number 3, then add another corner to it, its shape becomes a square which is the expression of number 4, solid and down to earth. From a metaphysical point of view, the addition of the spirit of 3 and the 4 of matter become 7 or when multiplied become 12. These two numbers – 7 and 12 – represent the governing of the rhythms and cycles of life, the universal energy. Hence, our 7 major planets, days of the week, the 12 signs of the zodiac, the 12 months of the year and the hours of the day, the 4 cardinal points, the 4 seasons, the 4 winds, the 4 elements, the 4 quarters of the Moon, and the 4 important Tattvic tides of the year that I described fully in my book, *Angels, the Guardians of Your Destiny*.

In another of my books, *Seeds of the Soul*, I mentioned that numbers are the real underlying structure of the universe. I described the 12 fold experiences of the radiant energy of the universe which are the aspects of the soul.

From the material viewpoint, number 4s are the builders who lay down a practical structure. They are the organizers and managers who turn the dreams and ideas of number 3 into reality in an intelligent and disciplined manner. Once you have visualized a project in your mind, you will know exactly how to get the job done to everyone's satisfaction. Number 4s have a great deal of patience, especially when handling intricate details, even if they become frustrating. Whatever it is that number 4 is handling, he/she will likely hang in there until it is right, but sometimes this number's tenacity tends to border on the obsessive. A negative trait, annoying to other people, and an intense doggedness may well cause number 4 to miss out on opportunities that come his/her way.

Number 4s very rarely instigate enterprises or projects unless there is a great deal of energy flowing from number 5 into the number 4. Number 5 represents freedom, which does not sit well with number 4 who tends to view it as irresponsible, but the flexibility of 5 works wonders in releasing some of the inhibitions and over discipline of number 4. With these two energies combined, then the structural basis of 4 and the imagination of 5, could bring great accomplishment and success. For instance, the original setting up of the banking system and the start of the development in the 1950s of credit cards, originally promoted to traveling salesmen for use on the road. (Salesmen are number 5s!)

When you make your own chart and find many number 4s you may recognize that you are very much an "earth" person with a total sense of reality. This means that you are not particularly creative, being more concerned with details, structure, and security. This, in turn, can make you too conservative, over cautious, slow and plodding, tending to be somewhat suspicious of strangers and innovations. Quite a drawback in life. In fact, you could use some creative friends who could bring more enjoyment into your life to help you become less strict, disciplined, and inhibited. You could certainly use more variety in your social life. Does this sound a bit like you? Number 4s and anybody with a name starting with D, M, or V seem to be designated as the hard workers of this universe.

Number 4s also tend to be perfectionists, somewhat rigid and stubborn in their approach to life, which makes other people feel hemmed in and restricted. Although you have a great deal of self discipline, a remarkable memory, are very intelligent, and can be totally relied upon and recognized for your sound judgment in your work and community, you can quite easily become narrow-minded in your outlook, having little tolerance for the shortcomings of others. Flexibility is something 4s need to develop along with compassion and understanding, rather than dominating people and situations. Somewhere in the chart there are bound to be other energy patterns that will lighten the heaviness of this down-to-earth practical number.

Number 5

Five is the number of movement, of change and adaptability, free thought, freedom of choices in life through using the senses of perception, awareness, and emotions. Five is an interesting many-sided number. It is masculine in energy (3 + the feminine 2 = 5), becoming the middle number, the central pivot between 1 and 9. It represents the 5 senses – seeing, hearing, smelling, tasting, and feeling, the five forms of matter. It is the flower with 5 petals, 5 pointed leaves, the 5-pointed star of individuality and spiritual aspiration and is purported to be the 5-petalled flower of the lotus of the Crown Chakra. Its shape is the pyramid corresponding to fire (number 3, the agent of the transmutation of 1 + 2).The base of the pyramid is square (number 4) and represents the earth, and the apex is the start and finish of all things symbolizing the 3-fold principal of creation : Body, Mind, and Spirit.

Number 5 is versatility, new directions, excitement, change, and adventure. These are the idea people with a great love of variety, always seeking mental stimulation and new things. These are essential for the growth of number 5s or the negative characteristics will slip into place.

If there are energy lines from number 5 to number 4, 5 can give the flexibility to 4 that it so desperately needs and 4 can help to balance the flightiness of 5. By now you should begin to see how numbers in the chart can influence each other, often relieving negative traits and enhancing the positive.

Resourceful, fun loving, witty number 5, friendly, inclined to be intellectual and adaptable to most situations also has its own negative traits, often ending up as a *jack of all trades and master of none.* They are attracted by everything that looks different and exciting, impulsively seizing opportunities but throwing them to one side if things do not move fast enough or they appear to have strings attached. They hate to be tied down, they become impatient with rules, laws, and conventions, and if they cannot find the freedom and variety they require, they can become irresponsible, inconsistent, and lacking in discipline.

Nevertheless, 5s are good company, talkative, amusing and clever, making friends easily and quickly. They can be bold and aggressive when they really wish to accomplish something. They will use all their resources – and other people's – until they have achieved their desire. Once done, they will move on to something new, but if *Lady Luck* or *Dame Fortune* has let them down, they can become boastful, sarcastic, rebellious, becoming an opportunist at other people's expense.

Another side of number 5 can show up in a surprising fashion if there are energy lines from number 9. The spiritual nature of 5 most likely will show itself with an interest in a variety of educational subjects, metaphysical writings, in religions of the world, meditation, or becoming deeply involved in the family religion or becoming missionaries. Number 5s indeed are interesting people.

Number 6

Number 6 appears to be harmonious with all other numbers. It is considered to be the perfect number – 1 + 2 +3 = 6. According to Genesis in the Bible, God's creation was completed in 6 days. I guess there was some help from number 4 to give structure to this creative idea to bring it into material existence. After all, what is the material force except trapped energy.

Looking back at the other numbers, we have discussed we can see that the conscious, caring feelings of number 2 are connected and applied to the material world in the practical shape of number 4. 2 + 4 = 6. Now, when these two numbers come together, we see the creative intellect of 6 becoming imaginative because the personal creativity of number 3 (3 x 2 = 6) has added its energy to 6. So, altogether, 1, 2, and 3 become the imagination and abstract thinking of 6.

The 6-pointed star of this number represents the 4 elements. The point upward equals the male energy, fire and air, and the downward point is the female energy of earth and water.

If you can't quite fathom how numbers get together and impress themselves on each other, don't let it faze you right now; it will become much clearer as we go along, chapter by chapter. What I have been describing is the metaphysical basis of all the numbers which show themselves in material form when applied to our different psyches. They cannot be ignored, even if you are not consciously aware of them.

Harmony, order, and family life are what 6s frequently reach out for, often to the detriment of their own creative ability. There is much empathy and understanding of other people, enjoyment in being part of the community, and more than likely gives too much of self in all kinds of relationships, not leaving enough time to develop inner desires and needs. This tends to be a major drawback; undoubtedly some people will take advantage of 6's charitable nature.

Number 6 tends to be rather idealistic, wanting harmony and peace in their marriage, home, and business life. They have a hard time coping with the harshness of the world, as they are the peacemakers wanting only to enjoy comfort, ease, and beautiful things. Love, health, beauty, and perfection are what 6 inwardly strives for, not recognizing how much close contact they have with their higher self – hence, outwardly, not quite enough recognition of the reality of the material world. When they do recognize their inner power, they often become the clairvoyants and healers of this world.

This streak of other worldliness can be harnessed into the material world with the development of their creative power – maybe in the area of abstract art or design. Time (number 7) must be allocated for self – not constantly for other people. If this is structured, then the energy lines from number 4 can help to bring these original ideas into concrete form. Number 6s frequently have trouble in finishing projects that are started, so a deadline should be set and time organized for self instead of giving time and pleasure to others. Number 6 could really use some energy and lessons from number 7 to help organize their lifestyle, to become aware of time, and learn to be punctual.

Number 6 people are usually warm, affectionate, responsible, and tolerant folk, but they do have negative traits if they are unable to express themselves creatively or if they do not recognize the love other people give to them, because they believe they are not giving enough of themselves. In this respect there is a limited outlook, (actually a negative trait of number 7) becoming obstinate and unreasonable. Excessive worries creep into the mind, especially over family members. They can become jealous, meddling, and gossipy, losing their charming, loving personality.

These are the numbers of the second triangle. From the previous triangle, number 3 created something. It was given to the mental department where number 4 says, "I build structures," number 5 says, "I bring change and versatility into the structure," and number 6 says, "I will balance the two and make something beautiful."

Now we move into the final triangle of this cycle where the spiritual bridge can gradually start to unfold.

Number 7

This is a mysterious and powerful number as it is the highest primary number, complete in itself and incapable of division by any other number except 1. Number 7 is a challenge to live with and even more of a challenge to describe. It is linked with the moon, the underlying cycles of life, and the rhythms of the universe. It is also time – significant periods of time stemming from the link with the moon which rules the tides and time of humanity – the cycles of life and death, growth, and decay. There is the waxing and waning of the moon as it begins, lives, dies, and is born again – its four phases. Its cycle lasts approximately 7 days, its month equals 4 weeks of 7 days each. If you add all the numbers of 1 to 7, they total 28 – the number of days in a lunar month.

Number 7 corresponds to a number of other things, like the 7-pointed star, 7 colors of the rainbow, the 7 notes of the musical scale, the lyre which Apollo gave to Orpheus had 7 strings and its music soothed the hearts of savage beasts. The Greek alphabet has 7 vowels, which had an important influence on numerology as the vowels are the containers of inner reality as against the consonants that indicate outward appearances of personality.

We also know of the 7 Christian sacraments, the 7 deadly sins, the 7 virtues, the 7 wise men of Greece, the 7 wonders of the world, and the Seventh Day Adventists. Then we have the 7 sleepers of Ephesus – 7 Christian youths who hid themselves inside a cave to escape persecution of their faith. According to legend, they fell asleep and their youthfulness was miraculously preserved when they were discovered some 200 years later.

Number 7 is recognized as completeness due to its connection to the inner rhythms of the universe. It is powerful in the use of magic and often appears in spells and charms. Apart from being complete, the number itself is numerologically a solitary. It cannot be made by the multiplication of any other numbers and it doesn't produce any of the other numbers when it is multiplied. It is regarded as a lonely, isolated number, which paints the picture of the character of one who owns the number 7.

The mystic, the introvert, the scholar, the philosopher, the occultist, the recluse, the quiet, thoughtful person who stays aloof from the hustle and bustle of the world: Any or all of these can be part of the number 7. Meditation and reflection on deep spiritual matters appeal to 7s who seem to have an intuitive grasp of the rhythms of the universe to which 7 is the key.

Number 7s can be hard to get to know. They are rather secretive, preferring not to share their thoughts. They are perfectly happy to be alone, and when the rest of the world imposes itself on them and causes stress, they will cut themselves off from others and retire into themselves to find their inner peace.

Number 7s listen to the inner voice, always searching for the mysteries of the universe. In fact, the keywords for the 7s are "I Seek." They like to plumb the depths of the mind, which gives the appearance of being aloof when a lot of the time they are deep in thought. Their minds are analytical, solving problems in a detached way, not allowing their emotions to get in the way or lead them astray.

They have a distinct dislike for the superficiality of the mundane world. They are constantly surprised by the shallowness of humanity, their lack of understanding, or their little depth of knowledge. This brings out their critical nature and they can become quite cynical of life. Some can become unfaithful, dishonest, and cruel because they are unbalanced, lacking the understanding of the world of reality.

Underneath this attitude they are surprisingly sensitive; there is actually a very warm heart that does not appear on the surface. In fact, some may have a highly emotional nature which they are incapable of showing; they have a hard time with words, explaining themselves.

A balance is required, the serious nature deserves fun. They could use some of the expansiveness of number 5 learning to understand people and their foibles. The wisdom and understanding they have of the universe should be allowed to come to the surface instead of keeping it within themselves. When they do, their advice, counsel, and knowledge will be sought by others, and in this way, both their spiritual and material needs will be fulfilled.

Number 8

The understanding of the number 8 is the connection of numbers 2 and 4 – the balancing of the duality of 2 in the practical way of 4, then using the energy to transform material reality into whatever is needed or desired. The knowledge number 8 needs to recognize is that matter – the material world – does not last. It is constantly in a transformational state. As human beings, we are also regenerating ourselves through the urges of the unconscious mind and soul which contain the seeds of our experiences. These experiences can stem from thousands of past lives and these seeds can easily affect our spiritual and material growth. The unconscious part of ourselves and its demands frequently direct our lives unless we learn to control it. The eminent psychologist, Carl Jung, said, "The unconscious is responsible for the individual's moral behavior patterns." Number 8 should be aware of the balance between greed and controlled charity and success or failure.

The figure 8 is the caduceus symbol of eternity, infinity, resurrection into a higher consciousness. It represents the eternal and spiral motions of cycles – the two circles of dualism in the material world – success or failure. It is also new beginnings.

Number 8 is a new beginning after failure, a new life after death, and in the Jewish tradition, a baby boy is named and begins his life as a real person on the 8th day after his birth.

In the Bible, Genesis mentions that 8 people survived the flood – Noah and his wife, their 3 sons, and their wives – who had to begin new lives. The ancient Egyptians continued this symbolism of number 8 by putting 8 people in their boats in honor of the 8 people who survived the flood.

Number 8 introduces a new dimension, being the first cube having 6 sides and 8 angles. Number 8s are offered the good qualities of number 4 in double measure, the idealism of number 6 yet an intense involvement in material matters along with the option of utilizing spiritual energies to transform the unconscious urges.

Many 8s have a powerful ambition to be wealthy and successful. There is shrewd business insight along with cool, analytical thinking. As long as there is perseverance and self discipline, there is potential for enormous success where dreams and desires can materialize into the physical world. On the other hand, there is also potential for failure due to sarcasm, intolerance, arrogance, and impatience with people considered to be their inferiors. If there is strong materialism and a desire for luxuries, there is the temptation for gambling, to acquire them quickly instead of steadily building and moving towards something better. A win or lose situation, once again indicates the success or failure syndrome of number 8.

Number 8s are natural survivors of failure as a general rule. Their rational thinking and philosophical outlook saves them from worries and anxieties and their organizational powers will put them on a new path towards success. Strong, self reliant, aggressive with a will power and drive to achieve further goals, they'll pick themselves up and start again.

These clever, intelligent folk are involved in trade, industry, and commerce. Earthly power and status fascinates them, often taking them into the business of world affairs. This may lead to the constant effort of achieving success in all matters at the expense of family and private affairs. If this is your choice, you will labor hard for great success and when you are finally successful, you will most likely be misrepresented and misunderstood on the one hand, but inspiring to people on the other, perhaps through your visionary powers. Always remember that people in power have enemies and enemies love to talk!

Of course there is the other type of number 8 whose weakness is having little faith in self, refusing to trust their hunches and inner self intuitions, believing they do not exist. They demand recognition, yet avoid responsibility. Stubborn, arrogant, materialistic, and thoughtless, they expect help from others but refuse to acknowledge their help. This type is selfish, self centered, reckless, and when things go wrong, they tend to become fatalistic, invariably blaming others for the failure. The generous, broad minded and forgiving nature of number 8 doesn't exist much in the lower type. It would seem that these people have far to go in recognizing the maturity of number 2, the stability of number 4, the ingenuity of number 5, and the generosity of number 6. These numbers working together lead to recognition of some description, both good and bad – the past experiences are spreading out for all to see and become more obvious with the patterns of number 9.

Number 9

This is another recognized number of completeness; it is the final number of this triangle and the end of the series 1 to 9. It is also noted as a complete number due to the fact that if it is multiplied by itself or any other number, it always reproduces itself. 9 x 9 = 81 = 8 + 1 = 9. 3 x 9 = 27 = 2 + 7 = 9, and so on. Here's an uncanny feature of this particular number. If a row of figures is written down, their order reversed then the smaller number is subtracted from the larger, the sum of the answer added together will always be number 9. Here is an example.

75136482, then subtracting (the number backwards) 28463157 = 46673325, added together = 36 = 9.

Nine is the end of a gestation period – 9 months for human conception. It is the end of the number system before returning to unity – number 1 – therefore, a symbol of regeneration. From a metaphysical point of view, it is the last triangle where the soul energy and spiritual consciousness gained from other numbers enters the conscious level. It appears to be the ruling principal. Carl Jung, in his book *Man and his Symbols* says, "For centuries number 9 has been considered a magic number. It represents form of the perfected trinity in its three-fold elevation." Note we are working with three numbered triangles representing this threefold elevation. I prefer to use triangles because their symbols speak of enlightenment. With their points reaching upwards towards the universal source of illumination, enlightened change comes from the understanding and use of the energy of numbers. The triangle is also the Greek letter Delta – the mathematical symbol for change – transition.

This is the completeness gained from true insight which brings the transformation and regeneration of the spiritual seeker. According to the Hebrews, it is the symbol of truth.

When 9 was used in magic, the magic circle was drawn 9 feet in diameter. Number 9, being the number of initiation, its cultural associations with secret societies can also be seen in some darker sects as pain and injury. Initiations into these societies frequently involves ordeals and mutilations.

Due to number 9's abstract concept of perfection, the owner of strong 9s in a chart unconsciously reach out towards this state. Like number 6, 9 wants to reach perfection and completeness in life and would love to transform the world. The idealism and compassionate nature of 9s leaves them somewhat naïve about human nature. They are not particularly good at judging the character of others, always seeing the best in them which leaves the 9s at the mercy of the selfish, greedy people who will take advantage of their generous nature. They will always be imposed upon.

Nevertheless, 9s continue to give to others in humanitarian and philanthropic ways without thought of return or reward. Many are metaphysically inclined and turn to the healing arts of Reiki, shiatsu, reflexology, acupuncture, aromatherapy, iridology, herbalism, homeopathy, or other esoteric forms such as healing hands. Any knowledge and experiences 9s have is willingly shared in an inspirational manner which expresses their own approach to life. In fact, they have an abundance of wisdom which is gained from experience rather than introspection. These are the true humanitarians who fight for social causes, the poor, the unfortunate, and the down trodden. There is a strong built-in desire to serve humanity.

These charming, idealistic, benevolent people may have had difficulties in early years and many of them will bring success into their lives through determination and resourcefulness. There is a high intelligence quota here, they reach out also for spiritual achievement, and their actions are inspired through intuition and inner self connections. The independent, very spiritual 9s tend to apply thought and logic to the principles of reality and then transcend them through metaphysical disciplines. These number 9s tend to walk alone, being masters of themselves.

Another side of 9s show them as impressionable, absorbing the emotions of others, tending to drift along with hardly any plans in mind. They also tend to be romantic, passionate, yet easily hurt, although you will rarely know if you have done so. The hurt doesn't last too long, as they fall in and out of love easily and frequently. They make friends easily, drifting from one to another with no true attachments. If they lack the boundaries of number 7 they can lose themselves in their dreaminess or by putting too much value on absorbing knowledge without sharing it with the rest of the world. This defeats the purpose of the spiritual 9 as the interaction of self with the world and other people eventually leads to an awareness of spirit.

Before we continue into the next chapter, there are two further numbers that should be understood as they will crop up in either the name pattern or the birth number or perhaps both. These are called the Master Numbers – 11 and 22. Sometimes they are condensed to a 2 or a 4; other times they are left with their full powers. Powerful indeed they are and somewhat of a challenge to handle.

Number 11

Number 11s are highly visionary, attracted to the unknown, inclined towards developing self enlightenment and spirituality. Somewhat like number 9, they feel that if they share their information it can "save the world." They are unusual, interesting people with attractive personalities, and when they share their teachings and inspirational insights, other folk feel completely uplifted just by listening to them. Part of their mission in life is to develop their leadership and share their knowledge, thereby proving to themselves that they can unite all aspects of their inner selves. In this way, they feel balanced and in touch with the energies of the universe.

This is a necessary part of life for 11s, as they have the inborn duality of the number 2 (11 is 1 + 1 = 2) that feels they need people and must be part of a group to feel whole. Number 11 is the leader of a group, not a follower like 2. It is a channel of the subconscious for ideas, intuitions, and psychic information which comes to them without conscious thought. Faith and acceptance of this ability creates a dynamic personality, yet peace, gentleness, and sensitivity flows at the same time.

Number 11s have usually been extremely sensitive and psychic since childhood. They have often "seen" or "heard" what others cannot, or have just known instinctively what is going on, what other people are thinking and their motives. They have understood in their later years that not everybody has this facility, and if it has been discouraged in their earlier years, shyness will have developed and an inability to express their feelings. Daydreams, a fantasy world, and not being able to tell the difference between reality and the imaginary takes its place along with vulnerability, and self created fears and phobias. The inner conflicts, nervous energy, and impracticality of the duality of number 2 has robbed the 11 of its greatness – all except its charisma.

If 11 can recognize this weakness of turning in on itself, what caused it and created unnecessary fears and lack of confidence, they should now focus their tremendous power on a goal beyond themselves, let their fantastic psychic and intuitive power start to flow again and their greatness will soon start to become part of everyday life.

Number 22

This number is another visionary, but this time with action behind the ideas. Number 22s are ambitious people who can turn their dreams into reality. They can visualize the archetype and along with discipline and self confidence can bring it into material form. Number 22s do not limit themselves. They have leadership, idealism within their plans and ideas combined with the practicality of number 4 (22 is 2 + 2 = 4) and the inspirational insights of number 11. They are often considered to be ahead of their time.

Like the 11s and the 9s, 22s also want to "save the world," but they do it in a practical, perhaps philanthropic, way. They tend to be in control of large organizations that benefit humanity and raise social awareness. They are often involved with world peace organizations, even missionary or charity work. Many of the younger 22s align themselves with organizations who are against nuclear weapons, irradiated food, genetic engineering, and also back the animal and human rights people. Somehow these 22s tend to meet up with the number 11 people, who give their help in roping in the lonely, idealistic number 9s in need of an all-consuming cause, along with the 11s who have become the wimpy insecure folk of the number 2s who will never be leaders, only followers.

With the number 22 being the number 4 raised to an extremely high power level, they are more inclined towards the professional world than the manual labor of number 4. Number 22 is the master builder, but they must have other people to give their aid to be able to accomplish things. They are full of ideas, unconventional in both thought and action, using common sense and business-like methods, especially if they get into politics.

They too have their faults. The major ones being lack of faith in other people's abilities, trying always to control situations and people, manipulating them to suit themselves. They can be selfish and petty. If their nature is impractical, they will hide from their own ambitions, being afraid to step forward and take the lead, wasting most of their potential. This leads to inner pressures, frustration, and a great deal of temperament.

As you can see, the energy patterns of all the numbers when combined or interwoven contain the essence of a person's name depicting the truth of character and the course that person's life is likely to take. This is the basic framework of numerology taking us into the next most interesting chapter where you can put together a simple chart of yourself by writing out your full name then applying the numbers from the alphabet.

Chapter 2

Your Name: The Key to Your Life

We've looked at each number separately and each triangle on a singular basis – 1, 2, and 3; 4, 5, and 6; and finally, 7, 8, and 9. These triangles represent the energies of action (physical), thinking (mental), and whole self (spiritual). The composite number of your name indicates the characteristics of yourself, your thoughts, feelings, and opinions that arise from the unconscious part of yourself. These are the invisible roots of our conscious thoughts. Many numerology books refer to these communications as the expression number. It is exactly how you express yourself to the outside world, while keeping your inner self well hidden.

If you are an astrologer, or have knowledge of astrology, you will recognize this expression portion of your numerology chart as the ascendant/rising sign of your horoscope. The addition of the numbers of the letters of your full name shows how you see life and how others see you. This is the mask you wear to the outside world and the vowels and the consonants describe your secret self, your longings and desires, which we will discuss in chapter 4. This area of the full name of your numerology chart indicates a specific path or journey of your life that can point you in the direction of self recognition, perhaps even total awareness of self and the world around you.

Earlier, I mentioned the name Claudia Holmes. Lets' get to work on her chart which we will use throughout the book. At this point, you can start the layout of your own numerology chart by following the construction of Claudia's. (If you are a married woman, I suggest you first make a chart with your maiden name. Read the information in chapter 3, Change Your Name, then make another chart with your married name. You'll see a distinct personality change.)

In the introduction, I laid out Claudia's name. She does not have a middle name, just a Christian name and a surname. Below is the alphabet with the appropriate numbers of the letters – you might want to copy it out and pin it on your wall. (See Appendix for a larger copy of this chart.) This way it makes it much easier for you to follow further instructions regarding your own name and life path.

1	2	3	4	5	6	7	8	9
A	B	C	D	E	F	G	H	I
J	K	L	M	N	O	P	Q	R
S	T	U	V	W	X	Y	Z	

Here is the construction of Claudia's chart and how I came to the total number of her name.

C	L	A	U	D	I	A		H	O	L	M	E	S
3	3	1	3	4	9	1		8	6	3	4	5	1

First name total = 24 = 6
Surname total = 27 = 9
6 (first name) + 9 (surname) = 15 = 1 + 5 = 6.

The full total of her name equals 6.

This complete number 6 is made up of Claudia herself being a 6 and her family name of Holmes totaling a 9. It is not just the Christian name of Claudia that has an impact on her; the energy of the family name – number 9 – also carries a different impact. The number and vibrations of the family name belong to a long line of Holmeses – father, grandfather, great grandfather, and back as far as you want to go. Whatever energy patterns – thoughts, opinions, morals – contained in this name have been handed down and absorbed by the receivers and then passed on to their children, which makes up the foundation of the children's lives. In other words, you follow the habit patterns of your father (which he had handed down to him), listen to his opinions, follow his suggestions, and most likely do as you are told. This has now become the framework of your own thoughts, ideas, actions, and responses.

Now, if we take apart the name Holmes, we start to see Claudia's foundation and why she responds the way she does.

Holmes is made up of the numbers 8 6 3 4 5 1 – notice the numbers 2 and 7 are missing. The character study we get out of these numbers which represent her father has an effect on the rest of her family as well as herself.

Studying the letter O, the first vowel in the name, we find a 6 indicating the father's love and concern for his family. In his eyes, all things should be harmonious and work smoothly amongst all family members. He will do his utmost to provide this environment, although at times he does upset the apple cart with his moodiness and sensitivity.

E, the other vowel in the name is a number 5 giving him the aptitude to handle many and varied tasks in making sufficient money to live comfortably. The H of Holmes, a number 8, points out his practical ability in handling business affairs, but the number 5 brings out some of his impatience and impulsiveness, which occasionally causes business and money losses. He also tends to invest unwisely in the stock market and other places through listening to the advice of others – number 8. Nevertheless, he bounces back, finding creative solutions to any problems he comes up against. These ups and downs happen periodically as number 2 is absent from his name. There is not much steadying influence to guide him.

The S in his name, being a number 1, propels him forward with a great drive for success. He prefers to work alone, has his own business (number 8) in the design field (number 3) as he is extremely creative and artistic. His earnings finally brought him the luxury and comfort that he has always desired but it has not always been so, due to his dreaminess – number 9 – and missing out on opportunities. He occasionally still has money losses, despite the steadfastness of number 4 of the letter M when he refuses to listen to his intuition and blithely goes ahead and takes chances. His thoughtlessness and careless action – the letter L, a number 3, has cost him loss of both money and friends in his early years when he was building his future. This brought unhappiness into the home, the one thing he wished to avoid. His failures and self recrimination bring on deep moodiness that affects his family as he reverts to aloofness and indifference, which was how he handled his own unhappy childhood of restrictions. He wanted to be an artist, but was denied the opportunity to go to art school. His family had always been accountants – number 8 – and he was expected and required to join the firm. The number 1 at the end of his name gave him the courage to go his own way forming his own design company which is a substitute for his strong artistic abilities.

He still handles money rather badly – number 3 – he is over generous, giving to people he considers in need without looking carefully at all the facts, and he frequently gets taken for a financial ride – this is the lack of number 7.

He was brought up with strict morals impressed on him by his father and grandfather, both of whom had strong religious natures that they forced on him. The overall pattern of the final total of Holmes as a number 9 eventually moved him away from a strictly religious household to more of a spiritual understanding of the world and humanity. With the pattern of his upbringing, he tends to philosophize, forcing his ideals on his family and dreaming about a utopian world. He wastes time, money, and energy in chasing this dream. He has a strong social consciousness, is very much an environmentalist – number 9 – and tries to force his interests onto the younger members of his family, number 4 – "father knows best" attitude .

If you look at Claudia's chart you will see she is quite rebellious, three number 1s. This is her unconscious reaction to this forced guidance she does not want.

As these are the invisible roots of our own unconscious thoughts you can see that they get there by being handed down to us from previous generations.

Having inspected her family name which involves her father and all he has handed down, we can now dissect Claudia's chart.

She has inherited her father's creative ability: There are three number 3s in her Christian name and one in her family name. She also has two number 1s in her Christian name and one in her family name. She lacks a 2 in her first triangle of physical action, nothing to join the 1 and the 3 together to propel her forward to *strut her stuff*. In other words, she has great difficulty in expressing herself, not only her creativity but also her feelings.

Number 1 says she is aware of herself and her creativity to a certain extent, yet she has difficulty in evaluating her self worth due to the lack of number 2.

With the difficulties she has in consciously expressing herself creatively and emotionally, her frustration causes her to be rather aggressive and destructive, (negativity of number 1). This is also a weakness of number 3 if initiative is not taken to express personal creativity. Because her father always insisted on knowing what was best for the family, it would seem her creative ability has been suppressed in childhood leaving her with emotional difficulties. It is interesting to note that she lacks the same number 2 and 7 as her father and he is doing to her what was done to him, yet he is unlikely to be aware of it.

With this lack of number 2 she has a deep longing for a profound – number 9 – close union. With the strong value of number 1s, she is somewhat picky and choosy about who she will allow to get close to her. She tends to drive people away, as she is very controlling and few will put up with that. This is her unconscious reaction to her father's control. She doesn't want control from males, so she takes charge immediately which puts them off. Deep inside herself she feels lonely and unloved – often a feature of number 9 – and she doesn't help herself very much by accepting what she thinks is her fate. This lack of perception of a spiritual dimension of her own special innate talents leaves her wide open to the shifts and changes of her material world. Her mind, body, and soul are uncoordinated. She ignores this feature of herself as she had her father's spiritual philosophizing thrust onto her as she grew up.

Claudia is actually an interesting creative personality. She really needs to give more time to herself instead of being involved in so many of her father's humanitarian causes, movements, clubs, and organizations – at his jurisdiction. This is so typical of a number 6 which is duty bound and takes on other people's burdens. This is mainly her own fault. Regardless of the fact that she doesn't like or want guidance forced on her, she leans heavily on her father (this is her lack of number 2) and relies on his guidance instead of organizing her own life the way she would like it. She lacks the discipline of building order and creative change into her life – this is the lack of number 7 – which leaves her feeling that life is dull and uninteresting which, in turn, brings out her negative judgment, from the number 4.

She also carries a further dichotomy around with her. One part of her wants a lover/partner, – number 2, marriage and children – number 6, yet she is desperate to break free – number 5 – and express herself in some creative manner.

Her thinking is unconventional and original – number 3 – in resolving practical problems – number 4. If she would listen to her inner self – number 9 – focus on the larger picture of her life and ignore the nitty-gritty details of number 4, she could come up with exciting and unusual creations that would carry her into the world of material attainments – number 8. Her tremendous creativity certainly deserves the light of day, if only she could accept it.

Was it fate or destiny that guided her to a decision to take up art classes? Whatever, it changed her life dramatically. As she became aware of what she had hidden away inside, her attitude to other people changed, especially towards the male sex. The instructor was most impressed with her creative output, encouraged her to really extend herself without controlling her in any way. Trust blossomed and into this trust walked Cody Michael Montgomery, taking art classes simply as a relaxation from his busy pressured days. Was he destined to fill the gap of her missing number 2? Will this relationship last a life time ... or ...? This is another story we will discuss in chapter 12 on love and compatibility.

Chapter 3

Change Your Name, Change Your Personality

You have probably gathered that Claudia's new relationship eventually brought her a change of name when Cody asked her to marry him. We shall get into that shortly by dissecting his family name and what effect it had on Claudia and her new life.

The majority of women take on the husband's name when they marry, but what about the people who want to combine their maiden name with the husband's name or people who just wish to change their Christian names? A name change should be carefully considered as well as the reasons you wish to change it. What is behind the decision?

The change you make by your choice of name or the joining of two names is going to make an impact on your outer life – your social and professional world. When you change your name, you change aspects of your personality because you exude totally different vibrations. It's not going to change who you are from the assessment of your numbered profile, but if you love the name you have chosen and feel different, then you will exert the positive energy of that name which changes your whole environment. What you give out to the world comes back to you in the same way that you gave out to it. As is said in today's parlance: You make your own reality.

The sound of a name is also an important feature. People react pleasurably or negatively towards it – especially if you have chosen the wrong one. For instance, how do you react to the name Patsy Sloots? Not a very charming name, pretty close to the word association of sluts; quite likely she was teased with it during her school days. Following her hearts desire to become an actress, it was suggested by Peter Noble, a gossip writer of the 1940s that she rename herself. She changed her name to Susan Shaw and quickly shot to stardom. Would the public have reacted in the same way to the name Patsy Sloots?

People really do respond to the sound of a name just as they unconsciously respond to certain colors – a like or a dislike. Strangely enough, the name of a fruit or vegetable can bring on a strong reaction, a love or a yuk: I hate that. I love carrots and cauliflower, but for years I wouldn't go near mushrooms. I had never tasted them; I didn't like the name. It brought on a sense of shuddering dread for me. What was buried deep in my psyche? Did I eat poisonous mushrooms in a past life that brought on death, pain, or discomfort? Who knows? My point is that you have similar reactions to certain sounds buried deep in your psyche that will appear at odd times for seemingly no logical reason at all.

Recall earlier I said a vibration is a feeling or an impression that someone or something gives off? Your choice of name will do just that, the vibration – the impression – will bring you friends or enemies, promotion or being passed over, attention when you require service, or just being ignored as if you didn't exist. You give off that energy pattern with your name, calling attention to yourself or none at all. Your name represents aspects of your personality. When you change it, are you going to enhance it or wipe it out?

Your Christian name or what you have chosen really is an important sound. On a surface level it tells people who you are. How your name is pronounced by you or other people – where the inflection is put – points to how you or they are feeling about either you or themselves at that time. This is an energy that is being projected and you will each detect how both of you are feeling when you meet or are introduced for the first time. Emphasis on the consonant sounds of your name reveals certain parts of yourself – those aspects of yourself you are willing to share with others. Interestingly, the parts of yourself you are willing to share will vary depending on who you are with, as you are already absorbing their vibrations and responding unconsciously to what you are receiving. In this way you are shielding your inner self, the vulnerable parts of yourself represented by the vowels of your Christian name.

I know this sounds a bit metaphysical/out-of-this-world type of thing, but if a dozen people were asked to give an opinion of you, you would receive a dozen varying viewpoints. Each person sees another side of you because you have projected a different aspect of yourself depending on the circumstances surrounding the meeting or get together. These are the consonants you project at different times and at different levels of your emotions. People do the same to you. As you learn and understand more about numerology, listen carefully to *what* people are saying and how they project their speech patterns. You will quickly learn to assess a variety of aspects within people and your own insight and intuition (number 9 in your chart) will tell you to respond, back off, or use caution.

Study yourself carefully before making your choice. Consult books of names for their meanings. There is an exceptionally good book on names called *The Hidden Truth of Your Name* written by a team of writers and editors that gives in depth profiles of hundreds of names. As you consult the meanings of a name, ask yourself if it reflects you – the whole of you – at this particular time of your life.

A lot of numerologists are hesitant about name changes. Personally, I believe a change is beneficial at certain times in our lives. My belief is that we gain a great deal of experience during the cycles of our lives, bringing portions of those previously described triangles to the fore and releasing what we no longer need; that's usually the end of a number 9 cycle. We've learned those lessons. We feel different, we're ready to take on something new and apply what we have learned in a totally different way. That's the number 1, the beginning of a new cycle. Why not go the whole hog, change names as well and derive the benefits of a brand new personality to go along with the brand new person you are about to become?

From a metaphysical and spiritual point of view, we are constantly "becoming." Nothing in the universe is static, and neither are we. When you recognize that you are "becoming" a new person (derived from the word personality), your spiritual sense has been activated through the energy pattern of number 9. You are living and working on all thrusters of awareness of the physical, mental, and emotional triangles. Listen to the messages of your inner self, see yourself as you wish to be, and "become" who and what you have visualized and created by your inner thoughts and desires.

We all have various tasks in life to accomplish at different times indicated by the missing letters/numbers in our charts. One of Claudia's tasks is to develop the aspects of the missing number 2 by asserting herself, taking charge of her life instead of being dependent on other people. She has three number 1s in her chart showing courage, leadership, personal drive, and creative force. To bring out these talents she needs to release this dependency/weakness of the missing number 2. At this time in her life, the end of a cycle was taking place (more about cycles in chapter 9). Psychologically, backing off from the guidance of her father and losing her dependence on him felt like an inner death to her, but the void it opened up brought about the freedom of some of the number 5 in her family name which boosted her awareness of herself, her senses, and her artistic ability of the number 3. The strength of her inner urges led her to the decision to take up art classes and that move opened up the future for her. Note that every action or reaction has a consequence and Claudia's action brought her talents and abilities to the fore.

Claudia developed confidence in herself and gained the strength of her own conviction of outward expression. The inner reaction to her newfound self helped her to tone down her aggressiveness and negative reaction to people, balancing some of her energy and improving areas of her weakness. The change in her personality through developing her courage triggered other energy patterns of the desire for lover/partner – number 2 drawing male energies towards her and her desire was fulfilled. Eventually, marriage changed her family name to Montgomery.

Let's see now what effect this name will have on her, opening up other avenues to a different life.

M	O	N	T	G	O	M	E	R	Y
4	6	5	2	7	6	4	5	9	7

4 6 5 2 7 6 4 5 9 7 total = 55 = 10 = number 1

The name Montgomery is missing a 1, 3, and an 8, but the addition of the numbers coming to a 1 makes up for the 1 missing in the name, so we are left with just the 3 and 8 missing.

The name Montgomery commands respect; it is a classic sounding name. There have been a number of well-known sports people, film stars, writers, singers, published authors (remember L. M. Montgomery who wrote the classic favorite *Anne of Green Gables*?), as well as the hero of the second world war, Field Marshall Sir Bernard Law Montgomery. (Interesting to note that his second name is Law – that is exactly the profession of Cody Montgomery, Claudia's new husband.)

Getting back to the family name and the energy patterns, morals, habits, and thinking patterns that have been handed down through the ages, we see from the first letter of the Montgomery name – the M which appears twice – a number 4, that family members can be utterly relied upon. When they give their word, that's it. Going right back to one of the early fathers of the Montgomery clan, Aaron started out in purchasing land and reselling it at a profit. He had an eye for a bargain, and with his hard-nosed negotiating skills and head for business, he made a lot of money, (the 4 + 4 of the double M totaling number 8, the money number, making up for the missing 8). Handing down his skills, personality, and religious thoughts (number 9), convinced that his daily dealings were influenced by the guiding hand from above, he encouraged his sons to expand into construction and contracting (number 4). Later, one side of the family went into manufacturing, the materials for the construction side, and eventually, they branched out into banking and investment. As their reputation grew, they moved into politics. The family members are philanthropists; they like to help people – a trait which has been handed down from Aaron as he never forgot how he was helped when he first started out as a young boy (number 6 and 9).

Despite the fact that the 3 and 8 are missing from the name Montgomery, it is still a very powerful and successful name. The 8 is actually represented by the vowel value in the name – you shall learn about that in the next chapter – indicating their success down through the ages in the business and monetary field.

The number 1 value of the addition of the name propels all the Montgomerys into action, pushing the number 2 to connect with mental energy of the number 5, which then activates the imagination and creative thought of number 6. And that missing number 3? The Montgomerys like their pleasure. It's not surprising; they are a hard working family. Most of them have a great sense of humor, they enjoy themselves to the nth degree, and waste quite a bit of money in the bargain. They deserve it and can afford it. They also give a great deal of money to various charities, museums, art galleries, and art schools.

I like the number 10 that the family name adds up to before being reduced to a number 1. It points out the intelligence, integrity, patience, and willpower that has been handed down to the clan from Aaron Montgomery.

Fame and reputation are written here for his various descendants amassing a good amount of wealth as long as they are cautious and very honest or disgrace can follow. With some family members in politics, that's a hard act to follow!

Many of them are exceptionally powerful and have dominating personalities; they are creative, original in their ideas, and have the strength of being leaders in any field they choose. They are extremely good at initiating new projects, leaving the small details of life to other people. They do have a tendency towards being stubborn and rigid about their own ideas, and they can become jealous of other members of the family whose ideas or accomplishments are on a par or even better than their own.

So what has Claudia married into? A fun-loving big family, welcoming her with open arms. The 2 that is missing from her name is bolstered by the 2 in the Montgomery name and the 2 in Cody's name, plus the consonant value of the family name is an 11/2, identical to Claudia's family name vowel addition. The balance number (more of this in chapter 5) of Claudia's initials – C for Claudia (3) and the H for Holmes (8) also totals an 11/2. She feels secure within this family, knowing now she need not lean on anybody. At last she is her own person. Her Christian name value adds to a 6 along with the Montgomery's double 6s and Cody's number 6 vowel value of his Christian name. She enjoys their intelligent conversations and the family's creative ideas have a lot in common with her own. She is missing the sense of discipline of number 7 and lacks awareness of setting limits for herself to stop her from spreading herself too thin. The family, especially Cody, will coax her in that direction along with helping her to find her own spiritual values – number 9 - which will come at a later date. She will not depend on Cody or the family now because she has found her own creativity in creating unusual beeswax paintings and imaginative sculptures from chicken wire, papier-mache and making the most intriguing sculptures using clay and lava rock. Her creations are starting to be sold world wide. Next, she is going to need the help of employees and she will need to take the step of learning to take control and become the boss.

Chapter 4

Vowels and Consonants: What's Missing?

The symbols we see that are the vowels and consonants representing your name involve more than just the combination of numbers for your whole name. Each individual letter provides a meaning of the material aspects of your life and also the complexities of your personality and your spirituality. Your thoughts and the intentions behind those thoughts – even if you are not aware of them – are eventually brought into your material world.

Every one of the letters of the alphabet has a personality of its own and each one makes itself felt in your everyday existence The ones that you see in your name are the ones you use in your outward existence, the missing ones are the weaknesses in yourself and also your hidden desires that only you know about and long for.

Recap

Just a little recap here to make sure you are still on track in deciphering your own name – or anyone else's name you have chosen to work with.

Your full name at birth and the addition of the numbers of the letters – just as we did with Claudia Holmes' name – represents your basic character and the personality you show to the outside world. This is the way you conduct yourself when you are involved with people, your job, and the daily situations you encounter.

Your surname numbers are the attitudes, prejudices, beliefs, morals, automatic actions, and responses you have inherited. These continue to be an unconscious part of the way you express yourself until you have had worldly experiences that have altered your thinking patterns and brought on a regeneration of some sort. This type of happening usually implies the start of a new life, a new cycle, with a different set of consequences for you to conquer.

When a number 1 year of a cycle starts, it brings many different types of opportunities for you to seek out to promote new essential parts of yourself. They can be anything from a promotion at work (or being fired!), to an invitation from a friend that brings a new acquaintance into your life. On a more abstract level, it could be a few words in a conversation, a passage in a book, or even something viewed in a shop window that triggers an opening in your awareness from your subconscious that sets you off on another path – a new journey in life, another adventure.

For Claudia, it was an advertisement in a newspaper that she rarely read that had been left behind in a coffee shop. She had ducked into it as a sudden cloud burst that brought on torrential rain. A chance happening? A coincidence? I consider these things to be synchronicity – thcy happen for a definite reason when the unconscious aspects of ourselves surface to consciousness and awareness of our innate talents spring to life. The time is right. The spiral of time is starting over again.

Recall the creative ambition I mentioned in Claudia's chart on page 38 which needed a kick start to put it into operation? The advertisement in the paper announcing the opening of a school of painting, pottery, and sculpture was the kick start. This was the trigger for the psychological breakdown of the original negative vibrations of Claudia's surname - the vowels O and E – that were holding back her freedom and creativity. Her decision to follow up on the advertisement activated three of her triangles (I briefly mentioned the major triangles on page 13 and if you look at Figure 1A in chapter 5, you will see a black line triangulating numbers 1, 5, and 9. This is her physical, mental, and innate talent energy rising to the surface. The dotted line at the top of the three triangles combines numbers 3, 6, and 9, a total creative line opening a door for her. The broken line triangulates the 3, 5, and 7, again increasing her awareness of her creativity, also giving her the recognition of having to put discipline into her life to achieve her objectives. The strength of her number 1 brought the start of her physical energy to life directing her to investigate the art school – the number 5 in her second triangle. This brought the empty number 7 into play to develop discipline and set limits of what she could comfortably handle. You will notice I have brought into play other triangles within the diagram . Within the nine numbers there are more than the 3 previously mentioned triangles; there are other horizontal and vertical dimensions that we will discuss in the next chapter when you learn to put your chart together.

Having taken this first step, Claudia was no longer Daddy's little girl relying solely on his guidance. She had gained a lot of experience during earlier cycles in her life, which she now realized had to be released if she was to use the strength and energy of her true self. Her weakness of dependency was being thrown overboard, and just like her father, who also has a number 1 at the end of his name (the S – remember the A, J, and S are all number 1s), she had the courage to finally go her own way.

So what's all this got to do with vowels and consonants? I mentioned on page 7 the vowels in your Christian name, the one you use every day (not your surname), contain your inner reality, the real you that would really like to see the light of day in all its glory. The missing vowels are the ones that are holding you back .These are the ones you must face, bring to the surface, tackle, and use them.

There are only five vowels in our alphabet to deal with: A E I O U. I presume you have laid out your name on a large piece of paper as you followed the steps previously mentioned? I am going to lay out Claudia's name with her vowels above her name and the consonants beneath. Do the same with yours.

		1	3		9	1	= 14/5 Karmic debt
C	L	A	U	D	I	A	
3	3			4			= 10/1

Her total vowel value is 14/5; her karmic debt (these are covered in chapter 6).

Her total consonant value is 10/1 (the same as the addition of the Montgomery name). Her first vowel value, an A, is a 1; her first letter value (consonant) a C, is a 3. These are her strengths.

Claudia's missing vowels are an E and an O. Yes, I know they are in her surname, but we are dealing with what is missing inside Claudia herself. What is in her surname relates to all the family members and each one will respond differently to the vibrations of the surname numbers. They all have different mind sets, differing emotions and strengths, different outlooks and goals. They are all different people.

We are working with one specific person now, all her aspects, strengths, and weaknesses; all her foibles, her certainties and uncertainties, all the things that make her a human being. If you recall the E (number 5) and the O (number 6) in her surname had a negative effect on her due to the protectiveness of her father. Her freedom of choice (E) was restricted. She had a large number of responsibilities placed on her (the O) relating to her father's involvements with a variety (number 5) of organizations (number 9) These two weaknesses would eventually have to be faced, whether through a crisis or an unexpected positive happening.

Both the missing E and the O are creative aspects: the E indicating she should make the effort to bring her creative talents out into the open, allow her emotions free reign in painting, sculpture, writing, music, dance, sewing, knitting, anything in the artistic field that appeals to her. The O, which is a number 6, the same value as her Christian name numbers, holds a desire for taking on responsibility, frequently taking on more than it can really handle. Somewhat traditional and conservative, like the 24 of her Christian name (that adds up to a 6), she allowed herself to be "put upon" finding her freedom (the E-5) only in creative *appreciation* instead of being the creative one. Quite a dichotomy, being pulled in two directions.

Although she has a U (a creative 3) in her Christian name, its energies tend to be unbalanced, rather like the number 2. Energies flow in, then out, scattering all over the place, and like the number 2, it desires to be supported. Look at the shape of the U, it has no base on which to support itself, it is an unsteady quality which would give no help to Claudia until she found the courage to support herself. Even the shape of the letters of the alphabet impose their energies on us indicating a meaning of the material aspects of our lives. The negative side of the U for Claudia pointed up her underlying uncertainties – her lack of confidence. She was afraid to take the step of expressing herself artistically in case she failed or made a fool of herself.

Looking further at her Christian name vowels there are two As and one I . The first and last vowel letters are the As (the number 1s). The first A represents a deep part of herself that few people ever get to see. Secretly she is more ambitious than she actually lets anyone know about, holding her desire for creative recognition close to her heart. These are her innermost thoughts. She wants to take charge and be a leader – of what she is not quite sure yet. In actual fact she is a leader, but in a negative way of being stubborn, willful, aggressive, and judgmental.

Deep down she wants to be independent, taking responsibility for herself and the career she would love to have. There is a great deal of strength in her chart especially in the first triangle within the creative number 3 and the physically active number 1. These two would eventually push her forward to grasp opportunities. Once a decision is made, she will take hold of her courage and push on with projects she has in mind until completed. This is indicated by the last letter vowel – the A. We saw earlier in the book how Claudia inwardly recognized an opportunity, grabbed it, and changed her life.

The other vowel, the I, corresponds to the number 9 in her chart. Once again this signifies the hidden artistic/creative innate talent. Sensitive, compassionate, and humanitarian she lacks confidence in herself and her abilities. The I and the number 9 stand for intuition, the 6th sense and imagination which she will develop and use when she has built up her self esteem.

The consonants she has in her chart – the C, L, and D – are positive energies which she will utilize when she has decided to take hold of herself and release her dependency on other people. The C can be very determined once it takes control of a situation. The letter L with the bottom leg pointing into the future will eventually lead her out of her self imposed restrictions towards the letter D which would open the door for her to walk through (which she did) .

In the meanwhile she had to contend with the missing consonants B, K, and T (the number 2s) and G, P, and Y (the number 7s) I'm sure you are beginning to see the negative and positive energies we all have within ourselves which bring us opportunities, failures, and successes if we can recognize them.

We already know that the missing number 2 in Claudia's chart made her feel dependent on other people. Despite the charm she has, she was also rather belligerent – the negative side – instead of getting ideas and plans together and putting them into operation to balance the energy flow. The missing K shows she has plenty of new thoughts and different clever ways of doing things. She has a great desire to get out and get on with life in a new way along with unusual relationships.

The missing T represents Time – when the time is right, everything would come together if it could be recognized and grabbed.

The missing G from the number 7 triangle says "not just yet." Claudia would have to wait (along with the missing T). Much is hidden inside herself along with all her secret desires. Even though she is very attractive and a social and fun-loving girl, she keeps her true self hidden. When she develops her trust, as she did with Cody, she will open like a beautiful flower.

The missing P from the 7 triangle says that she tends to keep her thoughts to herself; even in communicating with others she rarely reveals much of herself. When things get to be too much and frustration takes over through lack of creative self expression, she can be quite explosive – the bubble of the shape of the P occasionally bursts.

Finally, the missing Y which is also part of the 7 triangle brings a fork in the road at various times in her life, either forced on her or taken by choice. Note the shape of the Y. If she is disciplined and also uses her intuition, it will help to guide her decisions, otherwise she can become indecisive (the negativity of number 2) and somewhat confused. Isn't it fascinating how the numbers and letters speak to us?

Keywords for the 5 Vowels

Did you get your own vowels and consonants arranged and discover what is missing in your name?

Here are a few keywords of the 5 vowels to help you on your way and a précis of the shape of the letters.

A

Ambitious, leader, self starter, adventurous, independent, opinionated, stubborn.

The shape of the letter A suggests two feet planted firmly on the ground giving balance and self control. The bar in the center reinforces these energies adding initiative and importance to life's actions, perhaps even a bit too much self importance. When As run into problems, they become disturbed, upset, and confused losing some of the balance of the two downward points the A stands on. With the two points of view, they tend to dicker about making a decision: *What* shall I do; what *shall* I do? At this stage, it is best to decide quickly before losing total balance and control of a situation. A, being a number 1, can become quite selfish, self centered, and opinionated, looking out for number 1 and nobody else.

E

Freedom of expression, travel, movement, flexible, enjoys learning, speaking, writing, impulsive, restless.

The E, with its three prongs pointing to the right, always looks towards the future: change, freedom, openness, new experiences. The straight line the three prongs are attached to add to the upward movement of the mind, giving an interest towards spiritual and hidden teachings. The center prong is the balance between the spiritual and material world, but E being the 5th letter of the alphabet, puts all 5 senses into action with generally more interest in worldly matters than spiritual. Nevertheless, the Es are frequently very intuitive and rather idealistic.

I

Sensitive, intuitive, emotional, creative, artistic, humanitarian, can become a martyr, over compassionate.

This 9th letter of the alphabet – the end of a personal cycle – always indicates the start of new things on the horizon. For the Is, at first there will be tests and trials to be worked through with much wisdom being absorbed before setting out again onto the number 1, the next step.

I, this 9th letter, has much spiritual understanding and brotherly love to share. Its vertical line represents spirit descending into matter, and with nothing much to balance its shape, it can be very emotional and sensitive. Its major lesson is to master the self and the deep emotions, learning compassion and understanding instead of falling back on the ego of being hurt where no hurt was meant. Is are often more concerned with the self; then they become arrogant, and critical. The I looking like the number 1 is also an initiator. It starts and finishes and usually achieves its goals before moving forward.

O

Responsible, disciplined, spiritual, balanced, conservative, complacent, self satisfied, judgmental.

O, being the 15th letter of the alphabet vibrating to the addition of number 6, has a love of family and home. It also has an eye on money. O is a complete self contained circle, it is all or nothing, full or empty. Its opinions are very firmly fixed, it is possessive, holding closely what it has within its circumference; protective, responsible, conservative, and moody.

It is the shape of an eye and we see things with both the outer and the inner eye, absorbing and retaining knowledge from other worlds. Or we can close our eyes and pretend things do not exist. It is a magical shape, like a magic show – now you see it, now you don't. Its shape is also like an open mouth where the exclamation, "Oh, now I see!" pops out. Some Os can be jealous, self righteous, meddlesome, even becoming a tyrant, and very far from being omnipotent.

U

Creative, talented, intuitive, adaptable, receptive, scattered, impatient, unbalanced, needs support.

This 21st letter of the alphabet, adding up to the number 3 is shaped like a receptacle – a cup shape. It is open to receive everything that comes its way and sometimes spills out its contents through being greedy, jealous, temperamental, and selfish. The U does not have a steady base on which to stand. It moves from side to side, left to right, past to future, which shows up as indecisions and uncertainties. It becomes nervous or over emotional, then loses everything it holds in its cup. U's must learn to maintain a balance through self control. Because U is the 21st alphabet letter vibrating to number 3, it has much in common with the number 7. 3 x 7 = 21. 7s can be warm and spiritual, even overly religious or cold and materialistic. So can the U. Similar to the 7, it is usually quite conservative yet speaks well or, on the contrary, will remain silent and non communicative. These are the two sides of the U shape, a dual personality, and like the 2 (of the 21st) it feels the need for protection and a partner. If you turn the U upside down its shape looks like an umbrella and umbrellas always give protection.

Keywords for the Consonants

Now here are the letter shapes of the consonants.

B

Diplomatic, sensitive, kind, gentle, lacks confidence, needs others, belligerent

The number 2 of the alphabet in the shape of the letter B is recognized metaphysically as a house. This house is our body temple, the two rooms (the two circles of the B) house our soul and build the personality we show to the world through the power of our thoughts, words, and actions. The two enclosed circles on the vertical line of the B are where things are collected and stored in the shape of occult knowledge, ideas, or on a material-level items like a book or art collection. Bs remember and hold on to knowledge and memories. The top portion of the B is the spiritual side, under the dividing line is the physical world.

The two circles have another meaning. They look like female breasts pointing out the nurturing principle of B and the number 2. With its duality, it expects love and nurturing in exchange. Without it Bs can be secretive or sly and underhand.

C

Sensitive, intuitive, involved in the arts, sociable, scatters energies.

This third letter shape of the alphabet looks like one half of the letter O. Where the O's mouth is closed, C's is open, letting everything go in and out. It loves to talk – and gossip – for there is power in speech, pleasing or hurtful.

Cs are frequently scattered, show-offs, enjoying life and spending money. With this half moon shape and nothing to enclose it, Cs take in a great deal, then let it all flow out, even money and their emotions.

This letter, pronounced "see," in quantity in a chart, often makes a person psychic and clairvoyant. They are able to direct this unusual talent into writings and paintings and their unconventional ideas, received psychically, can be developed into the material plane earning them a great deal of money.

D

Responsible, practical, patient, honest, stubborn.

D, the fourth letter of the alphabet, is the door through which we walk, either in or out – through the metaphysical door onto the Path of Enlightenment or by shutting the door to keep out the unpleasant and unwanted energy patterns of the material world.

D is another enclosed letter where feelings of limitations or restrictions are felt. This is mainly because the people who have Ds in their name and number chart allow these feelings into their world by being over conservative. They make boundaries for themselves.

D is number 4 in the alphabet, 4 square, opinionated, workaholics, and sometimes rather dull. Ds need security, something to believe in, but the lesson they should really learn is to lighten up, let fun into their lives, open up to other ways of thinking and experience some of the wonders which lie within the universe.

F

Intelligent, reliable, stable, needs family and relationships, dislikes criticism, can be melancholy.

This 6th letter of the alphabet is not particularly well balanced as it has nothing much to stand on. The F has two outstretched arms inviting everybody else to bring their responsibilities and problems to them which they willingly assume. The negative type go overboard, taking on too much, so that they can play the part of the martyr. These are the people who frequently control their friends and family making an uncomfortable atmosphere.

The happy positive F with its two forward looking prongs looks to new approaches in life, has an open, intellectual mind and a 6th sense. Fs can be very passionate within the family environment and towards the people they really care about. They have a voice that needs to be heard – politics, counseling, teaching, or in another sense, in the areas of beauty, art, music, performing. In its own way this is also serving others by the joy and happiness it brings to their inner senses.

G

Introspective, patient, dreamy, imaginative, aloof, lacks confidence.

This challenging 7th letter of the alphabet resembles the hump and neck of a camel. The camel was well known for storing water and carrying valuable, costly merchandise. The letter G also stores a great deal of itself, including its valuable spiritual understandings, which it prefers to keep hidden. This letter is self searching, analytical, secretive, and likes to be alone.

You will note that the shape of the G is rather like the C but it turns in on itself at the bottom. Its tendency then, is to be reserved, strong willed, opinionated, wanting to find answers to all hidden meanings. It doesn't talk as much as the letter C who lets everything out, but when it gets around to talking it shares a great deal of wisdom, for it is a deep thinker and chooses the values of its words to uplift others.

This picture seems like a paragon of virtue but the other side of this 7th letter can show a critical, sarcastic nature who can use hurtful words when the balance of its energy is upset and at a low level. This is the time when it needs to be alone to restore the balance and become its own peaceful self again.

H

Methodical, perceptive, powerful, executive qualities, confused, addictive, escapist.

It is easy to see a ladder in the shape of the H, the 8th letter of the alphabet. Above the rung of this letter the space represents a window through which the eyes of the soul can view both worlds. We can use the white light of the universe to bring happiness and understanding to ourselves and others or we can descend the ladder to stand on the bottom half becoming hard and materialistic. Such is the power of the number 8. To quote the metaphysical maxim: As we think, express and carry out our actions (as above) so shall we receive them (so below). The cause and effect producing the karmic debt that we discuss in chapter 6.

We know that number 8 is swings and roundabouts – success and failure. The letter H has both feet firmly on the ground so it must use the window above the bar to look carefully at what must be done. A positive frame of mind and good judgment enhances the balance of the H and the number 8 to be successful and wealthy. The H is open ended so care must be taken not to give away everything that it has accomplished.

The other side of the H can be bad tempered, a tyrant, too demanding, and making judgments or jumping to conclusions too quickly. They can be selfish and cheap wads, far from being the humanitarian that number 8 and the letter H usually is. The words they speak are particularly poisonous leaving an energy pattern of hatred in the environment. Balance is especially critical for this letter.

J

Leader, cautious, innovative, optimistic, quietly ambitious, indecisive, critical, unemotional, lazy.

The letter J, with its tail facing to the left, looks back on the past to use the experiences in a useful, positive way in the present and towards future achievements. J, the 10th letter of the alphabet, is efficient, organized, somewhat critical, has an ego of importance as the number 10, with the 1 behind the zero pointing to self and knowledge of ones own talents. Like the number 1, they are ambitious, creative, accomplish their goals without relying on anybody else. Js are leaders, not followers, and do not like being told what to do. They draw on their own inner resources.

The number 10 of the alphabet implies that this person has been here before in other incarnations and is able to draw on memories and experiences of the distant past. The 10 also points to a new level of consciousness on the Path of Enlightenment, either religious or metaphysical.

The other side of the J can occasionally lose confidence in self because there is no real firm base to the J – just the curl. This causes procrastination. At the time of this hesitation, Js must be careful of making sudden, wild decisions. These are likely to end in accidents of some sort.

K

Receptive, friendly, adventurous, strong willed, discontented.

This 11th letter of the alphabet, with its vertical line and two forks reaching up and down, provides the ability to grab all opportunities available and to retain what is necessary to further their achievements. The K is a higher octave (vibration) of the number 2, so it does not rely on partnerships to fulfill their lives. Ks find unusual friendships/relationships, careers, and artistic expression. Their energy is unpredictable with the two forks going in different directions. The upper fork reaches out for the wisdom and light, uses its intuitions, higher awareness, and follows its hunches. The upper portion of the line and its fork looks like a V. This is what holds things together for the spiritual K. The downward fork looks like an inverted V meaning they are materially inclined, feeling that they have to work hard to achieve their desires.

Every number and letter has a negative side as does everything in life. K, this higher vibration of the number 2 (the 11th letter adds to a 2), falls by the wayside as it takes on the negative aspects of the number 2, becoming overly sensitive, dishonest, intolerant, and unsympathetic. Some practice kleptomania (unconscious thievery), others, deliberate stealing, then lying about it. Controlling the impulses of the lower self is important with the letter K as the 11th letter of the alphabet is sending the power of initiation to those who have Ks in their number chart. The offer is to balance the energies of the higher and lower vibrations to reach out for the spiritual light.

L

Action, charitable, balanced, kind, accident prone.

L is the 12th letter of the alphabet so we are back to a higher vibration of the number 3. 12 is 1+2 = 3, the creative expression. L, with its bottom line pointing to the right, is the stick that prods people onwards and inspires them to improve and make the most of themselves.

The L is sexual desire – the phallic symbol which is the life force that pushes all evolution and brings manifestation of that which is desired or needed. This 12/3 we discussed as the creative trinity in the description of the 1st triangle.

L has a loving nature, devoted to family and can be wildly, intriguingly, and unexpectedly romantic. Usually warm and loving, L can become rather aloof, cool, sarcastic, and critical when upset. Really, L should learn self control where emotions are involved.

On the other hand, L, with its firm base line, does not scatter its creative energies like the C and the U (the other 3s). It thinks carefully along legal lines before acting, uses its intuitions, which gives it good insights into the motives of other people. The mind of the L is open to the spiritual plane, giving it psychic awareness and occult or religious leanings.

Its negative aspects are lack of patience and fault finding, seeing both sides of a question, and being indecisive. If they feel held down by self-imposed restrictions in their own environment, they tend to take out their frustrations on other people in an unfair manner.

M

Logical, reliable, efficient, courageous, workaholic, hasty, quick tempered.

Here we have the 13/4 of the letter M – known as a karmic number. It's the 13th letter of the alphabet. Adding up to a number 4, it stands well balanced on its two feet showing a strength of character. Again we see a higher vibration of the original number 4 (the D) due to the V shape in the center of the M. This V shape opens the mind to ideas and thoughts from a higher plane which brings positive change whenever necessary.

Because of its orderly mind and exceptional memory, M shows great management ability, good in business with positions of authority.

Ms are usually quiet people knowing that in the quiet and peacefulness they can rise above the impact of noisy earth things and people and call for spiritual help when they need it.

If Ms do not use their spiritual energy, they can become careless, dull, cold, and unfeeling, leaving themselves feeling blocked as if they have to climb a mountain to get anywhere.

N

Change, movement, excitement, variety, adaptable, sensual, imaginative, jealous, covetous.

The 14th letter of the alphabet is an interesting one. Not only is it made up of two Vs, one upside down and the other upright, the number 14 itself adds up to a 5, and 5 is the balance point between the numbers 1 to 9. The number 5 refers to the 5 senses which we use in everyday life. This letter N vibrates on a higher level than the E (the first letter of the 5 vibrations) using the senses towards a more spiritual nature by controlling thoughts and actions. You will recall that the letter E and number 5 is impulsive, daring, constantly changing its mind and life patterns without sufficient thought. This middle letter N is far more balanced, adapting to circumstances with an ease and grace seemingly through listening to a higher consciousness.

The two joined shapes that represent the letter N point to both the material world and the spiritual world. The left side of the N – the V shape pointing downwards – invites all the gratification and sensual desires the mundane world has to offer which will be taken up by the lower appetite of the closed mind. The upper shape of the V is open and receptive to the true seeker of enlightenment. This letter is one of those energy patterns where the seeker of spiritual understandings will have the pleasure and delight of meeting up with a spiritual teacher when they have control over their 5 physical senses. There is the saying that "when the student is ready the teacher will appear." N, being open above and below, will experience many changes in life. It is also as versatile as the E, enjoying travel and freedom but in a much more controlled manner. This letter gives a subtle psychic awareness which guides the truly creative imagination, almost as if ideas can be picked out of the air. The ones who are reaching out for spiritual unfoldment will make use of these energies in a constructive manner. Others, who are still enjoying the sensual stimulation of their earthly existence will bypass meditation and continue to enjoy all the pleasures and annoyances of the number 5.

P

Powerful, influential, knowledgeable, shrewd, self absorbed.

This letter stands for power. It is 16/7, the 16th letter of the alphabet, adding up to a number 7 where the mind leans more towards philosophy, scientific matters and/or spiritual endeavors. The vertical line reaches up for something more than purely mundane existence. Its power is expressed in writing and speaking.

The circle at the top of the line represents the human head. Physiologically it is the pituitary gland. When this gland is awakened, our intuition opens up. We develop that "inner knowing," a sort of mind-reading ability, and the knowledge that is available from the universal mind is sucked up by the P and retained in the circle of the head. This is where our thoughts come from and the control of the emotions or lack of them dictates our power of speech – how we express ourselves. Thoughts are very powerful things, bringing both health and wisdom, or we can destroy ourselves (and others) in body and mind through employing negativity.

P is intellectually and mentally inclined, concentrates well, and achieves goals with great success. Its other side can be stubborn, opinionated, have a big head, and a closed mind – note the enclosed circle. They can also be possessive and insecure because the P has no foot rest. Without some form of spiritual awareness, there is moodiness and bad temper and the circle at the top will occasionally blow like a volcano causing shattered lives.

Q

Originality, energetic, intense, enigmatic, stable, short tempered, boring.

The 17th letter of the alphabet insists on the balance of the male and female forces that are contained in all of us – the physical and the spiritual, the active force and inspirations.

In metaphysical terms, it is known as the "mystical marriage," a blending of our consciousness with the consciousness and light of the creative power. The joining of these energies allows the soul to awaken and start its climb back to its divine status.

The Q is the circle with a tail for balance. The circle is the reservoir of cosmic mind stuff – the consciousness of the universe which we can tap into through our meditations. We can take these subconscious experiences into our outer world for balance.

Balancing ourselves is the work of our solar plexus situated in the center of our bodies. Positive and negative forces leave an impression on us in this area and Qs are very much aware of this. Experiencing a shock, being upset, angry, fearful, hits us in our stomach area making us feel queasy, painful, fluttery and nervous. Positive energies affect the same area giving us a feeling of joy, happiness, excitement, love and lightness. Q's tail of balance is very important and must be put into operation as they can be too spiritual or material, tending to go overboard in either direction.

This 17th letter adds up to a number 8 whose two circles, one above the other, point out the areas of the spiritual top and the material bottom – success and failure, or going too heavily one way or the other. Qs and number 8 are quite psychic and need to have an understanding of this force to use and control their inspirations and vivid imaginations.

In words (like quiver, quantity, etc.), Qs are usually followed by a U, and this letter can give little or no help to a Q as its cup has no firm base to stand on. If Q is feeling uncertain, it must find its own equilibrium from its mental and spiritual world. Meditation on its sun center – the solar plexus – can usually bring rejuvenation.

R

Tolerant, harmonious, humanitarian, peacemaker, over emotional, confused.

R, the 18th letter of the alphabet, adding up to a 9 is the number of brotherhood and unconditional love. The energy pattern of this letter and number is mainly concerned with spiritual unfoldment, material matters, and concerns usually taking a back seat.

The pineal gland, situated in the middle of the forehead is referred to as "the third eye." When it is completely opened, spiritual enlightenment supposedly takes place and all knowledge that is contained in the universe is available to us. The shape of the R goes along with this understanding to a great extent if you look carefully at it.

The vertical line is the body reaching up out of self for something more. The circle, like the top of the letter P, is the ability to think creatively, drawing into the conscious mind the knowledge from the universe. The leg pointing to the right is the ability to take this knowledge and information to move actively and steadily forward. The leg is attached to the circle suggesting a raising of the thinking patterns towards spiritual understanding. The enclosed circle will retain any knowledge and deep thoughts that enter this sphere, so this is where we can find writers, teachers, and leaders in the metaphysical field.

The vibrations of R and the number 9 is the completion of a cycle. For some who are truly involved in the metaphysical field will experience the tests of tolerance, compassion, and understanding in circumstances difficult to deal with. They will get their rewards in due course.

Others will fail their tests by letting uncontrolled emotions rule them: temper, jealousy, impatience, physical desires of greed and lust, teaching the metaphysical lessons for vast sums of money.

The true R and number 9 is a beautiful person who gives without thought of return and radiates sheer joy for others to share.

S

Strong feelings, attracts money, magnetic, energetic, impulsive, sly.

With the letter S we are back again at the third position of the number 1s. Remember that A, J, and S all vibrate to the number 1, but at different levels.

It's the 19th letter of the alphabet adding up to number 10 (which then becomes 1) – a new beginning – a choice of another path.

This particular number and letter strives for the perfection of the number 10, quite often making a success of their projects, but with the curves of the S there are frequent changes of direction in midstream, also changes of mind, which makes planning ahead a problem. These are detrimental to their achievements; so is their ego or asserting themselves too firmly.

This 19th letter, the 1 and the 9, alpha and omega, the beginning and the end, frequently starts another project or puts another idea into action just as the final details are put into place on the work in hand.

Like all 1s they prefer to work alone without interference. They intuitively know exactly what needs to be done, they get on with it and don't care what others think.

Look at the shape of the S. It is two Cs joined together, one facing forward, the other backward – past and future. The top shape is open to receive spiritual inputs, recognition of talents, ideas, and intuitions from this level. The bottom shape is putting all they have into the material world using their good memories of past experiences.

The shape of the S is also the shape of the human spine. Our spine is not straight, it is gently curved like the S. Right at the bottom of our spine lies the energy of the serpent of knowledge and wisdom – the Kundalini power that moves up and down our Chakras in tune with our emotions. This is the power that is available to us through our meditations.

T

Long suffering, restless, helps people, over emotional, easily influenced.

This letter is shaped like a cross with its vertical line and the bar at the top. It is the 20th letter in the alphabet, relating to the 3rd position of the number 2.

T and the number 2's lessons are learning to give and take, to give service to others, and controlling their emotions instead of employing the "poor me" martyr syndrome. This temperamental T should also recognize its stubbornness, impatience, and intolerance and become more friendly.

The number 2 looks for marriage and partnership and the bar at the top indicates the load it will carry through the difficulties it makes in any kind of partnership if it has a high-strung negative attitude towards the world employing sarcasm and cruelty. The other number 2s, the B and the K, do not carry a load on their shoulders as they do not have the crossbar.

The bar, of course, can act like a protective device when love is flowing from the T. Peace is important to both the T and its number 2. Within the peace flows the spiritual energy which is essential for this letter and number or it will feel burdened by the crossbar above the vertical which can block free flow of this energy.

V

Ambitious, loving, family oriented, efficient, tireless, unpredictable, greedy.

This letter is an extremely strong one being the 22nd of the alphabet. The 22 is the number of the master builder whose energy can be used both ways, for good and evil.

The V, being open at the top is inclined to be on the intellectual side with a good, strong business head. Where there is no spiritual or moral guidance, they can be unscrupulous, greedy, and thoroughly materialistic.

If this is the first letter of the name, leadership abilities come to the fore.They have vision, strength and willpower, directing their energies into any number of projects which they achieve over and over again. There is much nervous energy attached to this letter and Vs should really get into the habit of a daily meditation and quiet time to restore their output of energy. Quite a few Vs follow a metaphysical path. The uplifted arms of the letter shape are open to receive spiritual help and ideas, especially if they listen and follow their intuitions.

The other side of the V, the very materialistic person is involved only with the earth plane and fulfilling their many and constant desires – money being at the top of the list. As soon as they get it they spend it, looking around for more, feeling insecure until they replenish their bank account, then they can spend it all over again. These are not the loving family type folks; their interest is solely on themselves and their own pleasures and enjoyment.

The V does not have much of a leg to stand on, just a point directed into the material plane. This does not give feelings of security unless spiritual vibrations are understood for balance.

W

Charming, exudes mystique, self expressive, risk taker, greedy.

This 23rd letter of the alphabet is a close relation to the V, the previous letter. See how it is made up of two Vs, but it has two legs to stand on giving it a much firmer balance. The W, especially if it is the first letter of a name has a very sensitive nature, both the 2 and the 3 being emotional vibrations. Added together, the 2 and 3 become 5, so we are back again in the area of the 5 physical senses, this time at a higher level of universal energy.

There is still the freedom the 5 needs in order to cope with the changing aspects of the every day world. Many 5s who reach out to the two peaks that point towards the spiritual energies will have reined in their desires of the sensual pleasures and dissipation of the two previous 5s. The restless energy of the E/5 has been harnessed and balanced, channeled into the N/5 resulting in a wonderful character of understanding both worlds of spirit and human.

If you turn the W upside down it becomes the letter M giving it three points of steady balance. This reflects into the reliability, efficiency, and control of the 5 senses. This is the objective of all spiritual work, eventually leading to a change of consciousness.

X

Promiscuous, sensual, seeks pleasure, unrestrained, unfaithful.

It is a good thing we don't have too many people whose name starts or includes the letter X, a most controversial, unbalanced letter which needs a lot of handling. It is a most interesting letter when it is examined closely as it is open on all four sides absorbing everything that comes its way. It also makes 4 separate Vs and those influences will have an impact on this uncontrolled and unrestrained person.

Being the 24th letter of the alphabet its number adds up to a 6 that desires loving family life. Its animal nature side is very promiscuous, ignoring the consequences of its actions, more or less "X-ing" out close relationships of family life. It also "X-es" itself out of friendships and relationships through feeling bitter and seeking revenge against people who may, even unwittingly, have crossed their paths.

The X can cut itself down to size through its own attitude and actions. Then feeling intensely sorry for itself, it can go off in another direction in a wholehearted manner to improve the conditions of mankind.

It can be all spiritual or all material, rarely balancing itself. Because it is open on all sides of its shape, it is vulnerable to all experiences, open to any suggestions and new adventures as well as entertaining highly unusual ideas of life and existence. Getting to know an X person requires a lot of patience and understanding; in fact, it is an adventure in itself.

Y

Freedom loving, independent, pioneering, intellectual, indecisive, dislikes restraints.

Here is another letter that requires a lot of understanding. The Y is always at the crossroads. Which way? What shall I do? Which path is the right one to take? There are always decisions to be made.

This 25th letter of the alphabet may well have leanings towards the mystical side of life. The 2 and the 5 add to a 7 inviting spiritual involvement. Another point here is the vertical line reaching up and the two arms, again looking like a V, are asking for spiritual sustenance.

This letter indicates the deep thinker open to ideas from the universal mind when absorbed in the peace and quiet of meditation. In fact, people with a strong Y or as the first letter in a name have a distinct dislike of idle chatter and tend to wander off by themselves into the quiet. This is the influence of the number 7, the addition of the 2 and the 5.

The material Y will probably have an urging to get involved in something of a deeper nature. They feel something is missing from life but they tend to ignore the feelings because of difficult decision making and taking the first step.

Because of the two upper forks there will always be the problem of decision making. The lesson the Y must learn is to listen to the inner small voice, the guiding principle of the universe, then immediately make the decision. In this way, the right choice will always be made because it is the voice of reason from the inner planes.

Z

Peacemaker, trusting, compassionate, practical, headstrong.

Another strong letter here, the last of the alphabet, 26 in number shaped like a lightning rod. This letter and number is full of strength and vitality, just like the electricity of a streak of lightning. The Z person is also capable of using their own personal electricity to give comfort or to destroy. They always have a feeling of power and rarely fail in achieving their goals.

Because of the power within this letter and number which adds to an 8, if the power is used unwisely and negatively, it can and will, boomerang back into the person's life with triple the amount of destruction that was sent out in the first place.

Negative Zs are sly, deceitful, controlling people and circumstances for their own benefit, lying and exaggerating, and rarely share anything whether it is love, money, or goods. Greedy is their middle name.

The other side of the Z who makes use of the vertical line of energy has a hot line into the spiritual zones, receiving inspiration, energy, and constructive ideas. The number 8 influence produces a leader whose vibrations, speech, and auric pattern inspires others. In turn, the love and radiation from those around will help the Z person further along his/her own path of spiritual perfection.

The letters and numbers have a fascinating language of their own from which you can draw a picture of yourself. The words, shapes, and letters can show you who you were, what you are now, and what you can become in the future simply by absorbing what they have to say.

In the following chapter you can turn your mental key and start to unlock the door to the mystery of yourself.

Chapter 5

Unlocking the Mystery of Your Name

Before we can actually start to delineate the chart and get into the depths of our psyche, there is some more learning to be absorbed.

Look now at the triangle diagram in Figure 1 (see Appendix), and you will see the three triangles laid out, each with their numbers. From these, you will understand how the connections between the numbers and the energy patterns interact with each other.

In chapter 1 you learned the meanings of the numbers and how 3 numbers form a triangle. Each triangle represents an energy flow to different parts of ourselves. The first triangle numbers, 1, 2, and 3, relate to the body energy – the physical energy we apply to our choice of action or using the passive side of taking no action at all (number 1). How do we consciously feel about what we intend to do? Can we make a decision to utilize that energy or do we listen and rely on other people's input? (Number 2.) Are we capable of acting on our own decisions, bringing some sort of communication or activity into our material world, or do we let opportunities pass us by? (Number 3.) This is a path offered, not taken, just ignored.

The second triangle, numbers 4, 5, and 6, draw together our mind energy. These are our thoughts and logical or insightful approach to problems, our logical structured foundation (number 4); here is the researcher, the problem solver. When we use the deeper perception of the 5 senses (number 5), it will prompt the use of intellectual creativity and beauty, such as writing a book, creating a painting, composing a piece of music (number 6).

The third triangle, 7, 8, and 9, is our spiritual and soul energy. Number 7 is our awareness of time and the constant change of the material world. Our innermost thoughts and depth of feeling is number 8. Number 9 holds our hidden talents and soul energy that can be brought to light through the awakening and transformation of number 8 putting our soul energy to work in the material world (number 7).

Each triangle has three stages in an upward movement.

- **Triangle 1** = active, passive and union (the outcome)
- **Triangle 2** = logic, perception, insight (choice)
- **Triangle 3** = material world, transformation, hidden talents (enlightenment)

There are also three stages in a horizontal movement, again making a triangle. When energy from number 1 in the first triangle moves sideways to number 4 in the second triangle, it creates the beginning of a structure, a foundation, something solid that can be brought into the material world through number 7 (which is in the bottom of the third triangle), provided discipline and awareness of time is applied.

On the second horizontal row, numbers 2, 5, and 8 come together activating the conscious feelings into number 5 to produce an awareness of sensations, bringing on an urge to expand. In turn, this inner feeling and outward movement causes a regeneration, a transformation and growth of the unconscious mind of number 8.

The final horizontal row is creativity, between 3, 6 and 9. Whatever came together in the creative outcome of number 3 at the top of the first triangle is now given sideways to number 6 to intellectually beautify the concept. The thought patterns from number 6 open up a channel from number 9 bringing innate talents to light along with spiritual awareness.

There are two further energy lines forming diagonals from corner to corner. These are 1, 5, and 9 and 3, 5 and 7, which I mentioned in the previous chapter that are in Claudia's chart. Number 1 suggests becoming aware of the strength of self as the senses are awakened (number 5) to opening the innate talent lying within (number 9). With the Number 3, here we have a link of creativity to the mind (number 5) leading into the material world (number 7). In this way, the flow of energies connect through the material, mental, and creative levels, plus the physical, intellectual, and spiritual worlds.

Right now let's get you started on drawing up your own chart so that you can gradually unlock the power within yourself.

Take a sheet of paper and draw three fair-size triangles just like the diagram of Figure 1 in the Appendix. Now put in the numbers 1 to 9 in each separate triangle. Write your whole name under the triangles leaving space to write the vowel numbers above as in Figure 1A. Now write in the numbers of your name.

Down the side of your paper write the numbers 1 to 9 as shown, then look at your whole name where you applied the numbers to the letters. Count how many 1s there are and put that number down the side of the page beside number 1. Then count number 2s and so on, with each of the other numbers in the name. If a number is missing just put a dash in the appropriate space.

Now move up to the triangles. How many 1s do you have? Make a circle beside the 1 in the triangle and put in the number. Do the same with all the numbers in all the triangles. Where there are no numbers put a small cross in the circle. Putting these numbers into the triangles shows where the dominant energy is and is not – these are the strengths and weaknesses you have. From here you will be able to see where the energy flows connect with each other.

The Balance Number

Further on down the side of your paper, put in the vowel values and the consonant values of your Christian name as you were shown in chapter 4. Just follow the diagram step by step. Next write in the first vowel value of your name, then the first letter value of your name. These two indicate your strengths. Finally, add together the first letter of your Christian name(s) to the first letter of your surname and write it on your paper. The number you come up with is called your balance number. If you havc two or more Christian names, just add their initials to the initial of the surname; there you will find your balance number.

Claudia has no middle name, the C of Claudia, number 3, was added to the H of Holmes, number 8. The 3 plus 8 totaled 11, adding together 1 + 1 = 2, which is her balance number. Most interesting, as she is lacking a 2 in her chart, this is what she needs to work on to balance herself and her life. When she runs into stormy situations she needs to be less emotional, gather her strength, and take control to sort things out instead of running to other people. If you recall, her lack of number 2 is a weakness which she must learn to strengthen.

What did you get for your balance number? What exactly is a balance number?

There are times in our lives when we run into challenges or difficult circumstances that have to be handled somehow, especially when we feel totally stressed out. Studying your balance number will give you ideas and helpful suggestions in handling seemingly impossible or intimidating circumstances. Within that number you will find ways of using its influence to stay calm, centered, and finally balanced again. Allowing your emotional anguish to rule will affect your thinking, making you take rash action or no action at all when you should be helping yourself to find peace within your turmoil. So pay attention to your balance number and feel yourself bringing stability back into your life and your stress level will gradually drop away.

Balance Number 1

You know you have a great deal of strength and courage, usually doing and instigating things on your own, but when you run into problems, strife, or turmoil, this is the time to allow other people into your life to give you help. Although you are not normally in favor of people giving you advice, this is the time to listen and make use of it. Whatever troubles you are going through, they can see them from a different perspective and it is quite likely their advice and help will be valuable. So open up, express yourself, talk your problems through with family and friends before you rush out impulsively, acting forcefully, which you may well regret later. Remember: "A problem shared, is often a problem solved."

Balance Number 2

Courage is required here to overcome troubles and difficulties rather than running away and leaving them for somebody else to sort out. There is too much emotion here for you to be able to see how to handle the troubles and this is the time to stand back and assess the situation. You can't ignore them, this is a time of growth for you where decisive action is required. Blocking them out will only cause more pain, bringing on a further sequence of problems that will have to be dealt with. In fact, you are quite capable of giving excellent advice to others, so apply the same advice to yourself and put your emotions on hold. If you allow them to run rampant, you will do foolish things. One of your lessons in life is to stand on your own two feet and face the confrontation or whatever you have run into. Become your own person instead of relying on other people. There are plenty more frustrations to come, and the sooner you learn to control your emotions, the easier life will become.

Balance Number 3

When troubles and confrontation arrive for number 3, it puts a break on the expansive and expressive approach to life, causing a great deal of frustration. This is the time when discipline and focus are likely to fall apart. Don't let that happen; be calm, sensible, hold your emotions in check, and be more objective about the whole situation. Vulnerability has no place in seeking solutions to problems. This is a time to be thick skinned, invincible, and objective. If you see these problems from a different standpoint, you may find the outcome brings constructive change, making life very interesting with a payoff you didn't expect.

Balance Number 4

When problems arise here, you tend to allow your anger to come to the fore. This doesn't solve any problems; it simply blinds you to the true perspective of the challenge in front of you and points out that you cannot have things all your own way. The answer is to compromise and see the bigger picture. Also try to see things from the other person's point of view.

Has your strong sense of justice been violated? Then balance it out with forgiving the person who trespassed, have compassion and understanding for what is going on around you. Ah yes, a challenge indeed. If you can learn to apply these virtues when you run head on into troubles, strife, and conflict you will be surprised at the feelings of peace and harmony that will infiltrate your inner being.

Balance Number 5

When frustrating times arrive, this is often an indication of a structured change, perhaps in career or relationships. This must be handled with care and patience, not making a move until all sides of the conflict have been assessed. There can also be a tendency to try to avoid these problems and feelings of stress by wasting time and money in shopping, over eating, and drinking, but this will solve nothing. You will have to face them one way or another. You need to ask yourself why you are approaching the problems in a negative fashion. Do you feel your freedom is being restricted? By whom? Remember you are the one who allows things to happen, or allow people to take control over you. If you think you feel this fear, seek inside yourself for the answer to these conflicting emotions and other thinking patterns you may well harbor. Then look again from a different angle; know that you are a very creative person and the solution to any problem, strife, turmoil, or unpleasantness lies within yourself. The answer will rise to the surface the moment you allow your mind to relax. Be open and receptive to what your inner mind is offering and remember that we are what we think we are.

Balance Number 6

Many of these problems and difficulties revolve around home, family, and domestic issues, frequently due to yourself being unreasonable and obstinate, including being a worry pot. If you think you need solace, then you will have to handle the situation yourself without the help of friends and family. You helped to create the problems; now you must find the solutions in a responsible manner. Think about how the situation came about in the first place; look at all sides of it. Were you critical, opinionated, unforgiving, too possessive, or acting like a martyr? Did you express yourself as being uncaring, uncooperative, just wanting comfort and ease for yourself? Have you developed a creative outlet where you can express yourself and your emotions, removing yourself from your negative attitude? This may well be the answer to your problems. You are the peacemaker and an understanding person. Apply that understanding to yourself to see how to handle the situation; then come up with the solution.

Balance Number 7

When situations develop, there is a tendency to curl up inside yourself. You would rather not deal with the issue; you much prefer to hide from the problems. The way you handle stresses is to retire into yourself to find the inner peace which resides there. This is a great way to handle stress or problems of any kind, provided you apply the analytical approach in a detached way, thereby keeping your emotions under control. You are quite well aware that emotions can lead you astray, and if you dwell on the superficial situation or the paranoia of the mundane world that has been brought to your attention, it will bring out your critical and somewhat spiteful nature. Stand back and try to see the situation from the world of reality that others inhabit. If you apply your wisdom and understanding of the energies of the universe, you may well be able to solve the problems by discussing them and pointing out how a different approach can fulfill the material needs of those who have helped to create the issues.

Balance Number 8

What are the issues and what is the solution? Part of the solution is not to manipulate other people, but to be part of the group. There is a great deal of power within this number and also a tendency to take control rather than taking on some responsibility. After all, you are part of the problem, therefore, you have to take on your share of being the problem solver. The problems that erupt around this number are invariably concerning the material and business world, once again bringing change into the environment. You have power, creativity, and leadership. Listen to the concerns, suggestions and ideas within the group; make sure it is an open discussion and respect the opinions of others. Analyze what is needed, bring your own rational thinking and ideas into the group discussion. This may well bring about a new dimension of growth for all concerned. If, on the other hand, you consider yourself to be the only person capable of making the "right" decision, becoming stubborn, arrogant, unbending as steel, laying the blame of the problems on the doorstep of others, and refusing to accept your part in them, you can be sure that failure will be quite successful!

Balance Number 9

When an emotional crisis enters your life you will have to come out of your ivory tower and put your idea of perfection to one side. Unfortunately, you cannot transform the world or human nature, therefore, you must apply thought and logic to the problems which are surrounding you. Being somewhat idealistic and compassionate, you are not a particularly good judge of human nature, seeing only the good in them without balancing and recognizing their desire for greed, power, and recognition. There is a need for your emotions to be reined in, to be ultraconservative in your approach and suggestions, so that people and groups will not take advantage of you and your loving nature. No doubt you will "forgive them their trespasses." Try very hard not to absorb their emotions or you will be hurt. Be determined and resourceful in sharing your experiences and knowledge in an inspirational manner with the people who have instigated the emotional crisis. Your own approach to life may well turn the tide of dissatisfaction and the prejudice of the people you are dealing with. After all, part of your mission in life this time around is to share your knowledge with the rest of the world when they approach you.

Note:

The number 11s and the 22s are not used in the balance numbers. If you have these numbers in your name or your life path, use the descriptions of the balance numbers of the 2s and 4s. These will express some of the experiences that you will come across in your life. These experiences cause after effects, namely, change in one way or another. When we reach chapter 8 on challenges and rewards, the balance numbers will be extremely useful. Right now, let's get back to your chart to start the interpretation.

Chart Interpretation

Your first step in putting your chart together is to go to your *surname* and start writing out your family history from your vowels and consonants. See what is missing from both and make notes on your chart paper.

The way to get started is to consider what has been impressed on you as you grew up. Ask yourself some questions. Did you have freedom in making your own choices or were they made for you? If the latter, how did you accept them? Were you happy or unhappy about having your life ruled or did you become rebellious? Were you loved and sheltered, even over sheltered or perhaps ignored with feelings of being unloved which lead to social problems and connections at a later date, these having an impact on your relationship skills. How about your feelings involving social and family commitments? Think about your schooling, the rapport with your teachers. What was your father's attitude towards you and the rest of your family? What was your parent's relationship like? However it is/was, you may well have the same approach in your own relationships with people, which would have a bearing on your life.

How about your teen years? Shy or promiscuous? What about the guilt or fear of being found out over what you were doing that was forbidden or was against the rules and morals of society...then having to accept the consequences of those actions of the teen years that changed the direction of your life? Were there any crises in your life during this adolescent time? Study this time period – it is very important.

Switch over now and ask questions about your family and previous generations. You can see your father and grandfather from your own point of view, but how did your father see his father (your grandfather) and his grandfather? Their characters, attitudes, thoughts, opinions, morals, ideas, actions, ideals, and understandings of their particular lifetimes have been handed down over the many years and finally have an impact on you. So ask your father's opinion of those years, what he experienced, how he saw life, how he was brought up, and what was expected of him in those years which were so different from ours today. Then go ask your grandfather the same questions about his father and the life he experienced. All these questions and answers have shaped their characters and yours also to a certain extent. Finally, turn to your mother and ask her opinion of how she saw the different sides of her husband (your father), her father-in-law (your grandfather) and your great grandfather. Perhaps your brothers and sisters will give their opinions of the family from their points of view to round out the family picture. There are a thousand, thousand questions to be asked to fill in the picture of the jigsaw puzzle that is you, but if you find yourself judging people and events of the past, understand that people should be judged by the standards of *their* time, not your own.

As you read my words, you may think this is a pretty boring thing to do, but as you get answers to those questions, they will bring to light the answers to the questions you have been harboring about yourself. In actual fact, you will find it quite fascinating to build up this picture as you interpret your character. So think about your memories, your personal experiences, and circumstances that brought about the experiences and these will help you to a meaningful and personalized interpretation. When we get to chapter 8 on challenges and rewards, you will see that certain portions of your life are repeating themselves. Recognizing them and being aware of them in advance, you can handle them in a different manner and then experience different rewards.

Recall, you are doing an in-depth psychological analysis of yourself, so dig deeply into your psyche and find your many sides.

Having done this, now go back to the missing numbers and letters in your surname. Consult the previous pages for the interpretations to fill in a bit more of your personal puzzle. The missing stuff are areas of weaknesses, the weak links – what is undeveloped in your character. Concentrate on these and get to know both the positive and negative sides of the energy. These are the experiences that you will keep tripping over in your life, the challenges that you will have to overcome until you learn to handle them. Of course, once you have rid yourself of those, you have changed your life and your awareness so a new set will come along and you will play the game all over again.

Every number and letter shows up strengths and weaknesses and they will guide you to the self knowledge that offers you success, and the understanding of the freedom from the limitations we've set for ourselves – the number 7 in our charts.

Now is the time to connect up the numbers on your chart. Get out your pencils and ruler. Consult Claudia's chart and see the lines I have put in there (solid, dotted, and broken). See Figure 1A. You can also look at Cody Montgomery's chart (Figure 2) detailed in Chapter 12 – Love and Compatibility – for his energy patterns compared to Claudia's.

Note which of your triangles has the most activity. In Claudia's chart, you will see the activity is mainly in the first triangle at number 3 where she has 4 values in the circle closely followed by number 1 with 3 values in the circle. All her energy is situated there in the physical body line. When she puts her energies from numbers 1 and 3 into operation, they stimulate the other numbers and other triangles. The middle triangle is the mental energy line putting logical thoughts and imagination to work, and the third triangle is the spiritual world where transformation of the unconscious can take place.

Which number has the most values in which triangle in your chart? Consult the illustrations and note your strongest and weakest areas which affect your different life sections. Put your pencils to work now and draw the lines through the various triangles, vertical, horizontal, and diagonals connecting up the various energy flows.

With everything now in place you should be able to write out quite an intriguing delineation of yourself. The picture has come to life through the triangles and it would seem to me that we have been given a very interesting three-dimensional game to play and our playmate is the creator of the universe.

Chapter 6
The Lessons of Karma

Carrying on the theme of the three-dimensional game of the creator of the universe, we appear to have invested ourselves in a lifelong experience of a variety of lessons. By choosing to incarnate on this earthly plane, we have debts to repay and rewards to receive from previous existences which we probably don't consciously remember. As we go through the life we have now chosen, we receive joy and happiness and sorrow and misery all caused, it would seem, from our thoughts (the seeds) which produce words or actions that have a great effect on ourselves, other people. Our thoughts also alter the structure of the energy patterns surrounding us and the plastic energy of the universe.

One of the Laws of the Universe is called the Law of Karma. Its other name is the Law of Cause and Effect. What you give out (the cause) you will get back in triple measure (the effect). Simply put, good actions deserve and get rewards, bad ones get what is also deserved one way or another. To use a cliché: *You reap what you sow*.

The metaphysical concept of Karma has been handed down since time immemorial. Every single thought, deed, and action from our first incarnation has been registered on the Akashik Record – often referred to as the Astral Light – and also on our soul. The soul carries these from one life to another during its slow transformation back to Divinity.

The Akashik Record is a part of the light that is the Web of the Universe. The web holds the universe together. The name comes from the Sanskrit word "Akasha" meaning the primary substance on which even the minutest details of every existence and experience are recorded. These records are the storehouse of spiritual knowledge and can be viewed or recalled with training of the mind. Some people are lucky enough to be born with this ability – Edgar Cayce and Rudolph Steiner for example. You may also have briefly touched these records when you have had a déjà vu happening – a feeling that you have had an experience before, or you have memories of a place that you are visiting for the first time and yet it is very familiar. That's part of your past-life experiences written on the Akasha.

Where did it all come from in the first place? It all started with our accountable action on our first arrival on this earth plane. This was the foundation for accumulation of Karma and the first blemishes upon our soul. With little or no awareness at that time our attitudes, concepts, desires, and emotions – hate, love, selfishness, greed, spite, and so on – plus all the kindnesses we carried out put the first accounts of our behavior onto the Astral Light. We have shackled ourselves to the Wheel of Life that slowly but continually grinds around until we reach sufficient enlightenment to take control of ourselves, and our five senses, develop our spirituality, and step onto the path of Light to the Divinity.

These are the debts we have accumulated that need to be repaid at some time or another, not necessarily in the next life or even the one after that. You choose the appropriate time for one or more particular repayments to be made with your choice of parents, country, environment, religion, color, and so on that will provide the necessary background for lessons to be learned.

These lessons and how you handle them are what pays off your debt. Of course, you can screw things up if you don't recognize or understand what is happening. If you handle a lesson badly, you will make more Karma (a debt) for yourself which goes onto the Akashik Record so you'll have to pay that back eventually. Using your Karmic strengths – your first vowel value and your first letter value plus your balance number (this is your attitude or your approach to a situation) can wipe some of your debt from the record. This comes to you as a reward in life which you will enjoy.

Having explained that, the challenges in life are the opportunity to repay a debt followed by a time of reward. If you understand astrology, you will recognize the Saturn hard times followed by the Jupiter gifts and rewards.

You need to find your Karmic Debt numbers first and what they imply, then read about your Karmic lesson(s) and how you can apply them usefully and sensibly to help you towards stepping off the Wheel of Life.

The vowel values of your Christian name(s) are the Karmic debts. The accepted debt numbers are 13,14,16,19. Look at the vowel numbers of your Christian name(s) which you have noted on your chart. See Claudia's chart, Figure 1. The addition of her vowels is 14/5. Yours should read 13/4 or 14/5 or 16/7 or 19/1. You may have none, one, or more of these depending on how many names you have.

Don't reduce these numbers, just leave them as they are.

Now consult the meanings below, reread your balance number, then ask yourself if your attitude towards solving the debt problem is appropriate or if you need to change your approach.

Debt Number 13/4

You will notice that the number after the slash gives the basic foundation of the debt. In this case the 4 implies you are going to work hard to accomplish anything. There are myriad problems and obstacles constantly bringing a load of frustration. Number 4s always work hard and need perseverance and a dedicated focus to accomplish a goal. When that goal is attained, it is well worth the trouble. This is part of a pay back for using others in a past life, letting them do the work while you lazed around.

Thirteen is a very powerful number although it is usually looked upon with superstition. It is a constructive and lucky number in its own right being a combination of the number 1 of independence and leadership and the number 3 of inspiration and self expression standing on the 4 square of construction.

The negative portions of the 13/4 are giving up the goal under all the pressures and difficulties, becoming lazy, apathetic, and developing a poor image. Just concentrate and direct your energies into a specific direction utilizing all the positive and creative qualities written in your chart and you will find success will be within your reach.

Debt Number 14/5

The 5 in front of the slash is representative of freedom – not yours but the freedom you have stolen from others in the past. You have encroached upon their territory depriving them of their own self expression, harnessing them into what you wanted and demanded from them without giving any thought about how they feel. Neither have you given anything in exchange. This time around, you will be subject to constant changes, unexpected happenings, circumstances which will frequently be beyond your control and the consequences will be thrown on your shoulders.

Were you born on the 14th day of the month? If so, you'll certainly experience pay back time. With all the changes forced on you, many unwanted and upsetting, you will need to keep your emotions under control. Many times there will be the temptation to throw everything overboard, feeling that you can't cope with anything anymore, then go off and drown your sorrows in drink, drugs, sex, overindulgence, and wastefulness. That's taking a step backwards, adding a further debt to your record which you'll have to repay.

You really can cope with everything that gets dumped on you. Just take a look at the 4 of the 14/5 that suggests you use its symbolism as a support – a rock to build on.

Self-imposed discipline is the start. Use practicality and precision in your everyday life. Put order, system, logical thinking, and method to work for you which you can fall back on when turbulence takes place. Make sure that people see you and know you as being reliable, trustworthy, dependable, and honest. This is the important part of the 14/5 debt. If you build your character on these lines, people will come to your aid when problems and troubles devolve on your shoulders and seem too much to bear.

When change is forced on you, make sure you take it in your stride and keep your goal firmly at the forefront of your mind. Work quietly towards it and gradually your dream will come true in the most unexpected way.

Note well: If you glance again at Claudia's chart, Figure 1A, you will see her Karmic debt number is 14/5. Her vowel value when added together is a 5, the number of freedom, which her inner self (her heart) desired so much to enable her to express herself in some creative manner. You will recall that her freedom was curtailed by the obligations placed on her until she took control and propelled herself forward. Part of her debt was paid in this way, other parts of her debt would be repaid gradually through the changes she makes in her life and will continue to do so until it is time to vacate her physical body.

I have often found that Karmic debt numbers and the addition of the vowel values are the same, and they usually indicate what is at the deepest part of the person's soul and desire.

Debt Number 16/7

The 7 in front of the slash indicates the need to find the path between the spiritual and the material worlds. In the past there has been pride, vanity, ignorance, and an egotistical attitude towards others considering them to be inferiors – a somewhat self-willed, self-centered life.

If you are still strong willed and egotistical, you'll make life tough for yourself until you learn what true willpower is and how to direct it.

No doubt you've found strange things happening to you, plans that were all set to go crumbling at the last moment, perhaps the loss of your name, position, or fortune. Ah yes, life presents challenges to your plans, and if you've boasted about them beforehand you'll eat humble pie as you watch them fall apart until you learn to keep your ego in check.

At certain times in the past you have not been very kind to your lovers. You've had affairs with partners who belonged to someone else, then you've dropped them over the side when you've become bored with them, walking away without another thought for them. This time around you will experience deception and false friends, broken dreams, and through these and other experiences, you will learn the value of optimism and introspection.

Study your missing vowels and consonants which are the weak links in your character, then turn within yourself for guidance before jumping to conclusions or making decisions and commitments.

The 6 of the 16/7 suggests you have previously been unwillingly to assume responsibility towards your commitments or actions you have taken. This is the time to turn things around, take stock of yourself, put your willpower and determination to work towards a goal or a specific talent you possess while holding your ego in check. You will encounter spiritual energies in this life as you are mentally directed to step onto the Path of Light. You will find old ways, thoughts, and life styles changing for you, being destroyed, but new, interesting avenues will always open up for you. The key to this wisdom is to listen to and follow the dictates of your inner spiritual guidance.

Debt Number 19/1

The 1 in front of the slash says you will have to learn to be more cooperative, be more tolerant and less domineering. You frequently find yourself alone facing personal struggles and wading through difficulties with little help from others. That's your own fault. When help is offered, you quite likely turn it down saying petulantly, "I can do it myself." Inwardly, you are afraid your secret failings may be found out and exposed. If it happens, then you'll have to face these failures. Sometimes things come back to haunt us, but being exposed to the light of day, they can show us where we went wrong, It's a valuable experience for the growth of your soul.

The 9 of the 19/1 points out that love needs to be given out to receive the same in return and the number 1 needs that love. This is the unconditional love given to all without judgment of others' actions, failures, attitudes, or morals. A difficult lesson to learn. Where the 1 of the 19/1 is concerned with self and its material achievements saying "look at me, see what I have done all by myself" the 9 goes quietly on its way, gently pouring love and kindness wherever it goes. When you learn to accept others for who and what they are without judgment your debt will start to be reduced.

Having looked at your debts, which are your personal repayment, let's get down to the Karmic lessons.

Within the eons of time it has taken us to arrive at where we are physically, emotionally, mentally and spiritually, we have all, in various lifetimes, practiced greed, treason, passion, murder, secrecy, intrigue, anarchy, espionage, burglary, vengeance, assassination, brutality, and anything more you can think of against the other members of the human race. Karmic lessons then, involve relationships of all kinds from family, business, love affairs, friendships, casual encounters, even strangers who are just playing a "walk on" part in your life but are necessary for the scene that is being played out.

We've all been heroes/heroines, do-gooders, best neighbors, nice people in general, and we are rewarded for these past actions. We take them for granted, enjoy them, maybe even boast about them, then think no more of them. But, when it comes to the lessons and the not so nice or the rotten bits of life catching up with us, we look at the negative side, we moan and groan, but we don't stop to think of what we are learning from these incidents or what set them in action. Experiencing these happenings can be an uncomfortable, and for some, a turbulent, even a painful time. The pain actually comes from confronting an aspect of yourself that you do not like. Your emotional response is triggered from an inner recognition of some unpleasant action from the past that you carried out that has finally caught up with you. It's not the emotions that are causing your response, it's the *dislike* of the emotions that's the problem. This is the discomfort. You don't like feeling this way so you need to examine your attitude.

Stand back from this discomfort and try to pinpoint your exact reaction. Think deeply on it. You may find it is a habit pattern which requires some alteration in changing the negative energy into a positive stream. What are you doing or saying that provokes a certain response from another person or people? You may well put your finger on the problem which can then be eliminated with a change of thinking and speech patterns.

Just recall that however we think and then put the thoughts into action will inevitably move us onto a path where we learn something else we have chosen to experience. In fact, every choice of thought and movement we employ offers us an alternative reality. Your approach to this new reality can bring you pain and distress or comfort and delight.

Study the Karmic lessons written below, see how they fit into your life and where you need to make some conscious transformation in your relationships.

The Karmic lesson(s) you are learning this time around are found from the numbers that are *missing from your whole birth name*. You may have just one to experience or many depending on how many numbers are missing.

These missing numbers from your own chart should have been written on the left hand side. You will find them under the heading "number value from whole name." Look again at Claudia's chart, Figure 1A. You will see she has two numbers missing, the 2 and the 7. These are the lessons and the experiences she will encounter in her life until she can recognize and come to grips with the bonds, links, and ties she has unconsciously carried over from previous lives. If you will recall, her number 2 is calling for independence and her number 7 requires discipline from her.

Below, in more detail are the Karmic lessons.

Karmic Lesson Number 1

The missing number 1s in your name suggest that you were a rather weak sort of person sometime in a past life, relying on others to direct your life. These traits may well show up in this one, meaning you are not aggressive enough to reach out for opportunities that could enhance your lifestyle. Your lesson is to learn to trust yourself – make your own decisions rather than asking advice from others. How do you know that they are right in their suggestions for you?

Put your fears behind you, learn to become decisive when it comes to starting new things or ways of life, and develop the independence that true number 1s always have.

Karmic Lesson Number 2

Somewhere way back in the past you were a most uncooperative, tactless person, speaking your mind whenever you felt like it, regardless of the consequences. You also had a good time spending money on yourself, sitting around, wasting time while others did the work.

This lesson is to learn working peacefully with other people, giving help when it is required and learning to make friends. If you are shy and tend to stay in the background, open up, smile and people will respond to you in like manner. Be patient, cooperative with any detailed work that is asked of you. With this change of attitude companionship, friendship, and partnership will become part of your life and the lesson will be learned.

Karmic Lesson Number 3

In a former life you had a speech problem. You may have been completely mute, perhaps deaf as well, and many people were unkind to you with your disability.

Now, with little or no number 3s in your chart, you lack the confidence to speak up or speak in public. Your lesson is to take yourself in hand, develop your dormant creative ability, and express yourself in some form or another that appeals to you, rather than scattering your energies and talents. Try writing, just let the words flow. This way you can keep your work to yourself until you have built sufficient confidence in your expressive self, then take the step forward and make contact with magazines, newspapers, and publishers. Perhaps you will develop the courage to speak up or speak in public. You really can do it if you try. Deep down all 3s are creative at many levels.

Karmic Lesson Number 4

In a previous life you really managed to avoid hard work, in fact, any work at all if you could avoid it. You were lazy, disorganized, and a slob.

This time around you get all the detailed work passed on to you and you must learn to be organized, focused, and accept orders from other people. Try not to go overboard and get bogged down with too many details – number 4s have this tendency. Lighten up and enjoy life all round.

Karmic Lesson Number 5

Number 5s are seldom missing from a chart being the center balance between 1 and 9, but if there is only one value there, it is indicative of being afraid of change and anything new in one of your past lives.

You will need to work hard on yourself in this life as 5s are the lovers of freedom, change and excitement. If you find yourself lacking interest in life and other people's lives, you must open your mind, become curious. Force yourself to understand and absorb new things, and above all, your lesson to learn is to face the changes that surround you, go along with them, and enjoy your present existence.

Karmic Lesson Number 6

You ran away from responsibility in one of your past lives, abandoning home and family for your own self indulgence.

Your fear of being tied down has made its way into this life. The lesson to be learned is being a good, kind, understanding partner, and parent if you take the step into marriage vows.

It won't be easy, but lessons very seldom are. They only hurt when you repeat the same error over and over again.

Karmic Lesson Number 7

In a past life you jumped to far too many incorrect conclusions about people and circumstances that virtually ruined their lives.

This time around you need to develop the ability of analyzing situations in all details before attempting a decision. Your lesson is to train your mind, develop a true working technique along with tuning into your inner self for guidance when you need it. Your extra lesson is to balance the energy between the material and spiritual worlds.

Karmic Lesson Number 8

How incompetent and greedy you were in the business world in a past life! All the schemes and projects you dreamed up that came to nought through lack of understanding, wastefulness, and bad management; then corruption of public funds. Think of all the other folk who suffered financial losses through your stupidity, lack of organization and avarice.

You are here to learn the value of money management and organization this time around. Somewhere down the line you are likely to own your own business or be in control for someone else. If you have not learned these lessons beforehand, Karma will most definitely pull the rug out from under your feet and you will lose everything you have through making the same error as before.

Karmic Lesson Number 9

A cold hard-hearted person you were in a past life with feelings for nobody but yourself.

Your emotions are on a roller coaster this time around until you can rein them in, understanding why you respond to upsets and disappointments in such an uncontrolled fashion.

Your lesson is involvement with others, being generous with your time, understanding, and love. First of all, though, you must understand yourself, otherwise you will be in no position to help and guide others.

Having examined your personal self and found many surprises within your numbers, we can now move on to a deeper part of yourself and look into your choice of a path of destiny.

Chapter 7

Your Birth Date

Your Life Path Number

We come now to the most important part of the book. This chapter deals with your choice of destiny – the life path you have chosen for this time of reincarnating.

Here I would like to briefly share a little bit of metaphysical understanding before we actually get into adding up the numbers of your birth date. A more extensive understanding of the following can be found in another of my books, *Angels, the Guardians of Your Destiny*.

According to my spiritual understandings, before we reincarnate again, we go through a review process of ourselves with the Lords of Karma who help us decide which karmic debts we need to pay and which karmic lessons would be advantageous to our selves and our soul.

To begin with, they help us review the Akashic records of previous lives to see what good deeds we have carried out and what bad seeds we have sown that will need accounting for in future lives. The Lords are very kind and helpful in explaining our previous experiences and our reactions to them and what can be of benefit to us this next time around.

Having selected the experiences we need, we are then shown a variety of parents who can form the background for our start of the new life. Once we have selected the parents, the die is cast so to speak. Our name and gender is written in the record along with the appropriate birth date we have chosen. Eventually, our soul, who needs and guides these experiences, takes up residence in the new physical body and off we go to our new life knowing exactly what is expected of us.

That's what *you* think. But the fly in the ointment is that on the way to your new existence, you have to go through the waters of Leith – the gates of forgetfulness that removes so much of the memories of the inner planes and what you decided to do with your new life. By the time your physical existence has an impact on you, you have forgotten all that you came to earth to do. How you handle your life now is how you make new Karma and get rid of the old. Well, I did tell you that we are playing a very interesting three-dimensional game with the creator and it's up to us to learn how to be the winner.

The winning hand is the numbers of your name and your birth data. The previous chapters have taken you through your name, your personality, how you respond and react with the rest of the world and how you control your emotions to overcome your fear, anxieties, frustrations, and imperfections, and how you handle your angers and sorrows.

The bonus is the life path, your date of birth you chose to walk this time around. From these numbers you can actually see your choices, what you have done with them as you have applied yourself and your personality on the experiences and circumstances that you came up against. You can look into your future, make a conscious transformation of the parts of yourself you have discovered and disliked, then set out on a new adventure with further self knowledge.

Come with me now and surprise yourself even more with the valuable information written in your birth date.

Lay out your birth information on your chart, month, day, and year and add the numbers together as I have shown below. This will give you your life path number.

Follow what I have done with Claudia's birth date. Her date of birth was November 11, 1966. See Figure 1 in the Appendix. This is a difficult path she has chosen for herself. Only she knows the answer that may show up in the challenges and rewards which we will discuss in the next chapter.

November is the 11th month of the year, plus the 11th day of the month plus the year1966. Add together 11 +11 + 22 (1966 = 22). These are all challenging power numbers which will stand her in good stead as she learns to take control of herself and her life. All the numbers added together become 44, another powerful number, then reduced to become number 8. Her life path number is an 8, a powerful business number giving her the required boost to her eventual prestigious achievements as she matures. This also added more power to her number 8 in her third triangle as the 8 is missing from her Christian name, one of the weak links and part of a karmic lesson. The energy of the master numbers is most valuable at maturity. We've made our mistakes in youth and growing up, learned some lessons, and now we can put the wisdom and knowledge to work constructively throughout our mature years.

Consult Claudia's chart again, Figure 1A.You will see the vowel value of her maiden name, Holmes, is an 11, her balance number is an 11 (reduced to a 2) both pointing to lessons learned and lessons to come.

In the first 20 years of her life, she was using her number 11s as 2s, falling back on all the weaknesses of that number; it is missing from her chart. The 22 of her birth year was also applied as a number 4 – adding to the squareness of her life and the responsibilities she accepted that limited her own life and expression. Because she has a low value energy in her number 5, she was afraid of change (left over from a past life, her 14/5 debt). She was afraid to make changes in her life. This would knock out the dependency of her number 2 – this was her crutch. Her lesson to learn is the courage of her number 1 to become independent and rely on herself and build and strengthen her number 2.

At this point, check your own addition of your birth data, then review your original chart with your vowel value, balance number, and first letter value. Do you have a match with your life path number? If so, you will have extra strengths on which to fall back at the rough times in your life. So what is your life path number? Do you have any master numbers? When adding your numbers it is best to turn the month, day, and year into single digits before adding them or you may miss a master number.

Let's say you were born on February 14, 1966. February is the 2nd month, and the 14th adds to a 5 and the year, 1966, adds to 22 so 2 + 5 + 22 comes to 29 which then becomes 11. Here we have 2 master numbers.

Now, if we had added the 2 + 14 + 1966, without reducing them to single digits first, that would come to 1982 which, added together becomes 20, then becomes a 2 and we would have missed the master numbers altogether. Just remember to reduce your birth data to single digits first, check your additions again before reading the life path numbers below, then discover the path you have chosen to experience.

Now you can compare it with the character and personality of your name chart and see if they are working in tandem.

Life Path Number 1

The choice of a number 1 birth path puts you in the forefront of anything you choose to do, providing there are energy values in the number 1 slot of your name triangle. If the number 1 is weak or missing from your name, than you must double your efforts to become Number 1 in the eyes of the people with whom you associate.

Your path is to be independent – to show your independence and leadership, to initiate action to let others see your leadership qualities. Your destiny may well be to introduce new ways, methods, and ideas of handling old ways that benefits humanity. Naturally, you will have to battle to get your creative and innovative ideas across to more stubborn minds. Use diplomacy, stay with your own convictions, use a certain amount of aggressiveness if necessary to promote yourself.

Number 1 is the pioneer, one who will take risks, looks forward to new adventures, and enjoys doing things alone. Being the lonesome kind makes it difficult for number 1s to take on a personal, close relationship, but this is part of balancing your life path. If you are self centered, demanding to have your own way most of the time, your relationships will fall apart fairly quickly defeating a karmic lesson you are here to learn. These lessons always involve relationships of some kind. Many number 1s are inclined this way, self serving, over confident, and impatient with people who are slow and amiable.

Your birth path suggests walking the middle lane, employing as many of the positive traits as possible. If your chart is weak in the number 1 energies, you will have to learn to stand on your own feet, not depending on other people, then develop your hidden leadership abilities – if you have this weakness aim for self sufficiency and personal attainment. Once upon a time, way back in a past life, you could have been very egotistical and demanding, pushing people ruthlessly aside to accomplish your goals and greedy enough to take all the glory and acknowledgments even though they belonged to someone else.

This could well be payback time as you have chosen a number 1 life path; perhaps in your meditations the information will float to your consciousness. If so, the weaknesses of the number 1 should be well considered and these will lead you to understand your dissatisfaction with your current circumstances and you can make the appropriate changes. Consult and use your balance number and karmic lesson number along with your birth path number.

Life Path Number 2

Controlling their extreme sensitivity is a lesson the number 2s need to learn as it can get out of hand, resulting in childish pouting, sulking, and broken relationships. Refusing to look inside yourself, placing the blame for any circumstances entirely on another person or persons is straight pure selfishness. A great deal of the time *you* are the instigator of the upset because you want to control all the aspects that surround you, including the people who are closest to you. Another weakness is a hidden jealousy that the number 2 person is unable to recognize, and along with this is an exuding pessimism and negative energy pattern which is felt by others.

Number 2s need people, groups, to be part of the community, to be wanted, needed, respected, and loved. To achieve this particular status and be accepted as someone with the special talents of peacemaker, diplomat, and organizer of difficult tasks, you must learn to control your emotions and sensitivity and stop reacting to every little word and gesture that surrounds you. This is the first and most difficult lesson of the number 2 path. If you continue with the self-centered attitude of "look at me always being hurt and upset by other people," other people will surely leave you alone to stew in your own anger and resentment.

Please be aware and understand that people do *not* hurt *you; you hurt and upset yourself* by your own reaction. This is how you make your own environment. You are entirely responsible for your relationships, either the pleasure or the pain. This is an important lesson to learn if you are to achieve your goals and work with your soul, who is attempting to guide you along the spiritual path.

The wise ones who have recognized, understood, and conquered this devastating, life-ruining problem have discovered their own personal power. In controlling their own sensitivity and rearranging this imbalance, they have found their inner strength of being a person of note.

Their shyness leaves them, they become self reliant. To their surprise, they find they can contribute their own opinions and ideas within a group setting and also bring harmony and peace when conflicting and troublesome opinions arise. No longer do they feel the need to run and hide to avoid unpleasant situations they get caught up in.

Number 2, you are actually the power behind the throne if you will only recognize your enormous power and abilities. You are the peacemaker, the calming influence filled with compassion and understanding. When you stand up for yourself, you will receive the credit for the work you do. Your accomplishments will be recognized and you will be known as a spiritual haven for those who need counseling and guidance.

It would seem that your path in life is of a humanitarian nature, exchanging self indulgence for selflessness. Consult your balance number and karmic lesson number along with your birth path number for soul enlightenment and further guidance.

Life Path Number 3

Number 3s are the connective productive energy streams of universal power and life. To give and to share this creative ability requires discipline and commitment towards developing your self expression in whichever field you choose.

Number 3s are people persons, talking, listening, gesturing, mentally on the go, always welcome in any social situation, needing the stimulation from others to further their ideas and creative expression. This is all very well if this energy is used to create. It is a nice positive way of living life, sharing your joy and happiness with others, providing it doesn't take up the whole of your life, frittering away the fertile energy that you have chosen for this life path.

It's a great temptation to sit on a bar stool saying: "I'm going to write a fantastic book, make a great movie, paint pictures that will impress all the souls of the world." Unfortunately, *your* soul will not be very impressed with your frivolous and superficial attitude towards the treasures you have been given unless you can get your butt off the stool and carry out your intentions. If you don't achieve anything this time around because your mouth is running away with you, you will have to repeat this lesson in double or triple measure with even more setbacks.

No matter how positive and creative you are, putting all of yourself into your project, you will naturally meet up with problems, reversals in your plans, and other annoyances – that's part of life but your sunny disposition should carry you through them if you acknowledge them, then work your way through them without letting them get you down.

A weakness of the number 3s is being a bad money handler. If you are disorganized and lack the stamina to handle your responsibilities in a serious fashion, you'll find bills unpaid and forgotten, credit cards used up, and a low or empty bank balance. Partying with friends or lending them money is a sure way to end up with little or no money. Friends will also take off when they see the money tree has died, leaving you emotionally vulnerable and depressed. Cynicism and sarcasm is added to your moodiness until you can pull yourself together again and get back on your life path. For all your jollity, underneath you are quite a sensitive person which rarely shows on the surface, so it is not surprising that you feel very hurt when you are treated badly by friends you thought you could trust.

Having learned the lesson of squandering your money and talent in favor of being the life and soul of the party, you'll think twice about being a social butterfly again.

Your balance number, karmic lesson number along with your birth path number will help you to control the highs and lows of your life. It will also open your eyes to your tremendous creativity once it has been harnessed and directed.

Life Path Number 4

Unlike number 3s careless handling of money, number 4s favor a nest egg to fall back on should life enter one of its really bad periods.

You are the four-square builder, the foundation of any enterprise. You are organized, systematic, industrious, able to make firm decisions regarding problem solving. You work reasonably well as a team player when you have your own tasks to attend to, but you object to any interference from others about your decision-making policies. You do have a tendency to be rather rigid in your thinking patterns – you are right and the rest of the world is wrong. You very occasionally misjudge other people seeing only one side of them from your blinkered point of view. In fact, sometimes you can be quite rude and bossy, a strong weakness of number 4s that does not endear you to other folk.

If you really did manage to avoid work and responsibilities in a past life – which seems likely as you have chosen a number 4 life path, you may find yourself being a workaholic with the intention of making a success of your life, perhaps even to achieve prestige and fame.

You've certainly got the willpower to get yourself on the ladder of success, but do recognize that you can be downright stubborn. When you've made a decision, even if it's wrong, you won't back down. This doggedness is another weakness of number 4s that should be evaluated, recognized, accepted, and altered. In the lifetime that you went on the "me first, only me" spree, you weren't interested in making decisions, doing anything for others unless it benefited yourself. This time it seems, you are going to extremes in the other direction, making all the decisions, regardless of the outcome.

Your personal domestic life also comes under scrutiny during this life path. Even your marriage and close relationships are subject to being programmed in an orderly fashion. You control their lives by making decisions for them, which tends to inhibit their freedom. You may not be able to see this side of yourself. You only know that you are dependable, that you have a great deal of patience with family, and those you love who are close to you. You willingly take care of them or even finish what they have started. You might consider how they feel when they see that, once again, you have taken over. Examine your feelings and emotions; ask yourself why it seems to be so necessary that you should constantly be in control. Meditate on it, change yourself, lighten up, bring joy and happiness to yourself, family, and friends. Study the previous interpretations of the number 4, positive and negative traits, move on to your balance number, karmic number/lesson along with your birth path number. Take the qualities of your name number and step bravely onto the path you have chosen.

Life Path Number 5

Boredom, routine, and being restrained are anathema to number 5s. Freedom beckons in any shape or form whether it is movement, communicating in writing, speech, painting, exploration, risk taking, experimenting – anything that offers a challenge in the different areas of life. Don't forget dance. This is one of the most beautiful ways to express freedom. It is liberation of body, mind, and soul, bringing beauty, grace, expression, and upliftment to the public. The decision to become a dancer/painter/writer or an expressionist of the unusual requires total commitment and discipline. This is one of the lessons the life path number 5 must learn.

Early in youth you've probably spread yourself all over the place, not knowing what you wanted to do with your life unless your innermost desire was able to impress itself on your consciousness. This actually does happen for writers, singers, dancers, and painters, and there can be total frustration with life until the opportunities assert themselves and you can recognize and grab them, which opens the doors for you. Then comes the lesson of commitment and discipline; your soul breathes a sigh of relief and says, "Good, let's get on with it; then we can take the next step up the path of Light bringing happiness and joy to both of us."

I know I am a great one for talking about and bringing the soul into these life experiences, but that's exactly what you are here for. Life is not purely for the benefit of your mundane self. You are simply the container, the vessel, the temple for the soul to guide you through the muddy waters of an earthly existence, help you make restitution for past errors, which then boosts the soul further up the ladder of Light. This takes place through your intuition resonating with the energy pattern of your soul during your meditation/quiet times. Hopefully, you can pick up the inner voice and avoid blotting your "copy book" to make further Karma.

Listening to that inner voice can help you discover what you were in past lives and what you are atoning for in this one. Because of your great need for freedom, you may have been a slave at one time who had no freedom. Perhaps you were disabled and deprived of your independence. There can be many reasons for your choice of number 5.

On the other hand, you may have previously been a completely wild unrestrained character causing many problems for a vast number of short-term relationships that you picked up, suddenly leaving them in the lurch without offering any explanations. You didn't want responsibilities, only satisfaction of the five senses. This time around, trying to fix the past errors, you may have gone too far in the other direction wrapping yourself in stifling situations, restricting your naturally exuberant self. This will not fix any problems. A dull, unrewarding existence for you will make relationships unhappy and unpleasant for others. You are only repeating the errors – result, no expiation. Whatever the reason for your choice of number 5, you will find the answers within yourself if you reach out for the guidance of Light.

Life Path Number 6

This life path is known for its strong family vibration. It feels the need for caring, nurturing, and service to others who need to be cared for. Nurses, home care people, and psychiatrists often travel the path of the number 6. There is a distinct love of home, family, children, pets, and an inner desire to take on responsibility, but you should look very carefully at this inner desire as it may well have a large slice of the martyr syndrome attached to it. Again, you may be taking on too much responsibility, wearing yourself out, opening yourself up to allow your negative aspects to take over.

You see, you are the advice giver and when people ignore your advice and go their own way, you can become bossy, domineering, and outspoken, calling attention to their faults while ignoring your own. You have a need to feel appreciated, yet you expect too much of people – even from your own family who will see you as an interfering parent or partner. Recall that whatever life path we have chosen, it entails reducing a karmic debt, learning a karmic lesson, and these are always involved somehow with relationships. Consider carefully the obligations you choose to take on, learn to say "no" without any feelings of guilt.

Turn to yourself, look at all the creativity you possess, then use it so that you can appreciate and love yourself instead of giving all your love to others.

You are artistic and vocal in many ways. What would you like to do with your talents? Sing? Then be a member of a choir or a singing group. Teach, counsel? Give time to *YOU*. Use your artistic sense in ways that please you. There are many ways to use it from cooking and baking, flower growing or arranging to needlework or painting and decorating. There are a hundred or more other ways to lose yourself in the joy of your inner self love. Give willingly to yourself what you so willingly give to others. Share your talents, show them off and note the admiration and appreciation of your gifts. When you have accomplished this, stand to one side and view yourself from a different standpoint and note the changes that have taken place in your life and relationships.

Life Path Number 7

So you have chosen the spiritual, mystic path this time around. Now you are a reserved, analytical deep-thinking person compared to a previous life for which you are now atoning.

I wonder what you were in that life that now gives you the need to be alone in this one, enjoying and needing the silence and the peace of meditation. Crowds, noise, commotion, loud music, loud people you cannot take and you vanish into the quiet as quickly and silently as you can. You are not a "party person."

The spiritual side of nature is the balance for negative conditions. We all have some negative traits so we have to see them, recognize them, accept them, and willingly alter them to bring in the balance.

Number 7's negative traits are based on fear, which can make them incessant talkers of nothing useful. Number 7s can be irritable, letting their emotions run away with them. They can be lazy, not finishing projects that have been started, and this, of course, kills all the inner creative aspects of which 7 is very capable.

Some 7s can be cold, calculating, lording themselves over others. They can be religious zealots and dictators, somewhat oppressive, unreasonable and full of resentment.

On the positive side of the 7, and you should consult the 16/7 debt number, you will recognize the spiritual energies you have inherited that help you overcome the destructive things in life that come your way. Being a 7, they most certainly will creep up on you when you least expect them.

If you have stepped onto the path of Light, you will have trained your mind to analyze situations thoroughly before coming to conclusions. Deep inside, you understand that lessons from the past can serve you well. Combined with your intuition and inner guidance you will develop the inner strength to share the depth of your metaphysical/spiritual understandings through talk or writing. In your silent and meditational time you have opened yourself to the mystical and the unseen, absorbed the information, analyzed and applied it logically to the material world, offering your knowledge to the spiritual seekers when the time is right.

You are usually a fairly silent person, but when you do speak, you have spiritual wisdom to share. People who are ready, really listen to what you have to share; they take your words to heart, apply them to themselves, and change their lives for the better.

This, then is the path of the spiritual number 7.

Life Path Number 8

This is the number of transformation. Which way will this transforming power work – into a solid material world of money, status, and success or applying the balance of combining it with spiritual endeavors? You have most certainly brought executive ability with you this time around. You are a leader, an organizer, capable of directing large businesses/organizations, even into the area of politics in the position of governor.

There is nothing wrong with being a good part of the material world – it's a fascinating place to watch with all its machinations, providing you don't fall into the trap of making more Karma for yourself with the greed that goes on. Note the scheming, the crafty plans, the conspiracy plots, the intrigue, that is carried out in the name of money making. This is the dark side of human nature, the selfish, material-minded, ambitious, goal-oriented folk who will achieve success and status at the expense of others without any feelings of guilt. The other side, the one of Light, encompasses having their share of the good and positive material resources through the understanding of their own personal power, compassion, and being part of their community. A feeling of compassion is the requisite for the control of their power.

Control is a very strong aspect of this number and it can be used either way – through greed and control of the resources of others, then eventually losing everything they have, including their reputations, or by understanding and using the spiritual energies that will manifest material benefits in equal measure.

A balanced number 8 is definitely on a life path of material, monetary, and emotional benefit. Within the community they are well respected. Positions of power and authority are offered to them such as mayor, bank manager, governor, or some political seat if that is the desire. Your ambitions, goals, and efficiency carve a rather nice niche for you. Your schemes and ideas, even of a far-reaching nature are eagerly accepted and you have the tenacity to follow them through to completion, benefiting a great number of people, including your own bank balance.

You fully understand that whatever you contribute to the material world, you receive back in unexpected fruitful ways from the world of the unseen. After all, what we have here (below!) is just the mirror image of the Above, where it all came from in the first place. It just spirals on around and around and what we request through our own actions is given to us.

In giving so much of yourself you must remember your home and family. Number 8s tend to be the over-working type, forgetting to express their love and warmth to their nearest and closest loved ones. This can be a pitfall causing a minor karmic debt, so do remember to get family involved – picnics, athletic stuff, boating, walking, whatever the whole family can do together. Put that time aside for them. When you are tempted to say, "no, I have work to do," have another think and tell yourself "tomorrow is also a day."

Consult your Karmic lesson, debt number if you have one, and your balance number along with this life path. You might also look at your missing vowel(s) that indicate your deepest desire(s), for this number 8 is a major number for altering the energies in your favor for your next incarnation.

Life Path Number 9

We come to the end of this particular cycle of numbers and number 9 is imbued with all the different energy patterns of the previous 8 numbers. Number 9 can see no faults or wrongness in anyone. In the spiritual sense this is a valuable asset, but once again, a balance is required by becoming a good judge of character, seeing through the wiles of those who would take advantage of this gentle, kind, humanitarian soul.

Financially and emotionally, you are liable to be hurt and you will pay dearly one way or another for your soft heart. You have your own personal needs and you must take care of them first. This is important for a healthy survival. Right at this very moment, look at the missing vowels in your chart, take note of your hidden desires, work on them to bring them to the light of day and the fulfillment of your self. You need to understand that whatever these inner desires indicate, they are the motivating factor behind the choices you are making and about to make.

Think deeply on yourself in your meditational time. See if you can pick up any tendrils of a previous incarnation that you may be dealing with now. If you avoided giving help to others that time around, you may be tempted to give too much of yourself in this one. These are the sort of things that leave an imbalance and eventually have to be corrected.

Wherever you go, you unconsciously offer love and kindness. It shows in your bearing, your attitude, and your friendliness. You are quite a magnetic character and being so interested in people you make friends easily, leading quite a social life.

Although you crave personal love, your love affairs do not last long. You are romantic, idealistic, and passionate, but your real true love is aimed at spiritual achievement and oneness with the universe, yet you have not yet learned much emotional stability. You have no real attachments to this earth plane, and if you do not recognize and utilize your talents, you will likely dissipate all your hard-earned energies. The negative side of this number, if you are just drifting, is becoming egotistical and conceited when you are with people, being also quick tempered, rebellious, intolerant, impulsive, and insensitive. This is a total turnaround from the positive number 9. Seeing and understanding both sides of this number is part of your lesson to learn as you walk this life path.

You really need to take stock of yourself. Reel in any over emotionalism you have towards people and this mundane existence – remember you are not a particularly good judge of character – then direct those feelings towards the artistic, literary, and philosophic fields. You have a great deal of spiritual knowledge earned through experiences of many lives. Rather than giving away all you have, you can share this with true seekers on the metaphysical path in the areas of teaching, healing, writing, or professor of philosophy, and whatever area you enjoy and become involved in, be sure you receive material benefits to compensate the outpouring of your spiritual energies.

If you do happen to have the life path numbers of 10,11, or 22, think seriously about the power they hold. Much will be asked of you in this life, both materially and spiritually, and great strength will be required to work through the heavy challenges you will experience. Your rewards will be in equal measure and spiritually they will be ecstatic.

Number 10, of course, represents the beginning of a new set of experiences on a higher mental plane than the previous number 1. The 11 and 22 are the master numbers with powerful energy. Some will use them as they are with all their strength; unfortunately, many who have these numbers will be applying them in their lives in the reduced state of 2s and 4s.

Life Path Number 10

I referred to the number10 briefly in the discussion of the Montgomery name in previous pages. You can't miss the number 10 people. They are exceptionally powerful with a commanding personality. They are individualists, intensely original and creative, good at initiating projects and they are perceived as always reaching out for perfection. It is actually the inner spiritual essence – the sense of perfection carried over from the number 9 that surrounds you. This is picked up by other people and some will emulate you.

In selecting the number 10 life path, much is expected of you. You are intended to use your artistic, spiritual, and inspired ideas towards the upliftment of humanity as a whole. You are the pioneer, the inventor with a rare leadership quality in whichever area of life you choose to apply your abilities. You are efficient, determined, ambitious, and your greatness is likely to come in later years where the completion of your ideas are manifested in the mundane world. Stick to your ideas and convictions. You have the inner resources to carry them through, seeing them through to perfection – that's what the zero cipher stands for. Actually, you enjoy dealing with challenges and obstacles, for you find a building of your physical and inner strength takes place, urging you on to develop your mind and leadership.

In the early years of your development, before establishing yourself you have had to be a follower, which didn't sit well with you. At that time you have shown your stubbornness and your impatience at having to be dependent on others. If you have been too impatient and too early in trying to establish your independence, you probably have been seen as self serving, selfish, and egotistical. Having to put up with your dislike of routine and detailed work during those establishing years has given you the experience of feelings of depression which actually has stood you in good stead for your later years. It would seem the destiny of your life path as a number 10 is to become sensitive towards the feelings of others and to understand their needs and requirements. This is especially significant if you are in the fields of law, counseling, or social services. With the 0 in front of the1, the spiritual essence of that cipher will flow from you to other people leaving them with the knowledge that they can rely on you for the help and guidance you give and they in turn will unknowingly fulfill your need of spiritual loneliness.

Life Path Number 11

Readers who are already on the spiritual path will probably recognize the shape of the number 11 as being the two pillars of Boaz and Joachim that stand at the entrance to the Temple of the Mysteries. These pillars hold the veil that must be torn aside for the seeker to enter. These mental pillars represent the positive-negative, masculine-feminine energies – the active and passive forces of nature and the universe. With our spiritual understanding of these forces, we bring a sense of balance into our lives. This is the Way of the Path.

Number 11 is the higher vibration of the number 2. Two, as we have already understood, is the follower, the dependent one who has a need for a companion or a partnership. Not so with the number 11. This life path stands on its own, taking the lead whenever possible, always wanting to give something to the world. Number 11s are usually professional people, teachers, counselors, artists, philosophers, performers, composers, musicians – music is an important and strong influence in their lives for its soothing and spiritual qualities.

Like the number 10 life path, 11s also strive for perfection. They seek the light of reason and understanding, to balance their dual natures through the inner wisdom and the understanding of self.

Intuitive, inspirational, idealistic visionaries, 11s are the deep thinkers, wanting to know more and more of the mysteries of life and the unseen. They frequently have a great knowledge and understanding, often far beyond the grasp of others. Nevertheless, they wish to share it because they are people oriented and humanitarian by nature. Number 11s are unusual people. Their broad-minded views intrigue and inspire whoever they come in contact with. This is where the balance for the 11s comes in.

You must recognize that you cannot keep your head in the spiritual clouds all the time, you have to come down to earth and deal with all the difficult or traumatic events that surround you. Rather like the astrology sign Aquarius, you must always keep one foot firmly on the ground while pouring out the waters of wisdom. You may have to learn some rational thinking which is part of the lesson of the life path 11.

There are other types of 11s who couldn't care less about the spiritual side of this number. They are still rather idealistic but instead of sharing it with their fellow men they tend to love the ideals instead. These are dreamers rather than doers. They have very little understanding of human needs, they can always verbally supply a universal remedy without recognizing or understanding what the other person needs. These types of 11s act out life through the energy patterns of the number 2, utilizing most of the negative side. They express their likes and dislikes quite forcefully, erupt into rages very quickly, dissatisfied with progress in life or their lack of it, and they are unable to control their nervous tension.

There we have the life path of the number 11 with its positive and negative sides. The higher the life path numbers go, the more difficult the experiences become, but that's your own choice as only you and your soul know where you stand on the spiritual scale.

Life Path Number 22

Whereas the really positive number 11 is a very metaphysical and spiritually minded individual, the number 22 taps into this source of energy. It utilizes the creativity and imagination and brings it into manifestation on the earth plane. In other words, what is there in the archetypal plane of the universe is tapped into through the mind of the 22, visualized strongly and the image is finally brought into the physical world as an object of some sort. The number 22 is named the Master Builder or Architect. The lesson of this number is to create and build either physical buildings/structures, innovative devices of some sort from their creative ideas that are used by fellow human beings, or to devise programs of spiritual or material benefit that does the same thing.

Naturally, there is the other type of 22, who ignores the ideas that crowd into their minds. They have no intention of becoming deeply involved in anything and no desire at all for any type of responsibility. Their own existence is of major importance, so they will act like an immature and negative number 4.

Even the most positive 22s can be stubborn at times, becoming both spiritually and materially destructive, going to extremes which makes life difficult for themselves. I doubt if any of us can be even tempered all the time; we need to let off steam somehow. The 22s are very sensitive people, they have an unusual amount of nervous tension usually directed into constructive projects. Being emotionally controlled helps in the business world to get their ideas into motion, and also keeps their love life on an even keel.

It is important for the 22s to get a good education, to use that wonderful brain power in practical endeavors. If education is not available, there will be feelings of inferiority, aimlessness, and frustration. Some will go to the other extreme of unethical and immoral behavior in amassing a fortune, controlling and manipulating people for their own benefit. They can be narrow minded and repressive. Luckily, these lower types of 22s are few and far between.

All in all, the 11 and the 22 work hand in hand although they are probably not aware of it. The 11 is the spiritual disciple with the same imaginative and creative streak as the 22. Everything they do is approached from a spiritual point of view. The 22 has the same intuitive, creative approach to life but is guided from the unseen to bring the treasures of the universe into material and practical use. Here we see the metaphysical law of *As Above* (the 11) *So Below* (the 22), bringing the balance of both numbers simultaneously into operation.

Chapter 8
The Challenge Experience

If life was smooth, easy going with no ups and downs to move us along, our existence would be terribly boring. The challenges bring us excitement and learning experiences, although we may not recognize them as such at the times of adversity;, and when the rewards come, we seem to take them for granted without understanding what the universal energy has given us.

The challenges are the times when some people appear in our lives who only have "walk-on parts." These are the folks who briefly cross our paths and seem to get the ball rolling for some bigger event that's on the way for us. They are the irritants, just like mosquitoes, which we have to bat away. When they annoy us or put our backs up, we invariably respond to them in some disagreeable or antagonistic fashion, opening the door for the real challenge to play its major part.

We all have different responses to these annoyances; it is an automatic habit pattern which we have developed. This is a weakness we need to become aware of and the challenge number will point them out for you to tackle and overcome.

There are four challenges in life that have to be faced and dealt with. They start at birth and end with death, and in between are the times of major happenings or crisis. They are always with us, hovering in the back ground, and during their quiescent periods is when we run into those minor irritants here and there, heralding something in the wings waiting to pounce.

Nice things happen to us more or less just before or just after the challenges are over. These are the rewards, called pinnacles in other numerology books. There are also four of these. They are long-term cycles on our life path taking place in between the challenges. We battle our way through a challenge of some sort, come out the other side and find we have a reward waiting for us. There are many different types of rewards, depending on your reward number. We could experience a most delightful uplifting interlude that enriches our lives or we could achieve a major success in some area. Perhaps we have overcome a fear, recognized a hurt we have been nurturing for years and released it, handled a difficult situation to everybody's benefit, headed off a major disaster with great diplomacy that has brought recognition. Whatever has happened, through these periodic negative and positive experiences we learn needed lessons and our rewards bring us great benefit.

How much benefit we get depends on how we handled the challenge and what lesson we learned. Did we learn anything? Or did we go ahead, ignore the lesson, commit the same error again and again continuing on with the same habit pattern we have established over the years that we will have to overcome and get rid of in future lives?

What the universe is saying is that if you didn't get the message of your weaknesses from your character/personality analysis, the challenges are giving you the opportunity to become aware of them and transform them into strengths.

Looking at the creator's game board; it appears to be your move!

At what age these cycles take place depends on the challenge and reward numbers derived from your birth data. If you have already been training your mind and your awareness, you will probably recognize what's on the way at the various times you will now work out for yourself, so you will be prepared for the event.

To find your challenge numbers you will need your Life Path number handy for the final stages. If master numbers come up in your calculations you must *reduce* them to single digits. You might also have your balance number close by in case your challenge number is being difficult. These combined forces working together could give you some help and relief in easing tensions and restrictions.

To find the challenges write out your month, day and year of birth. All calculations are *subtracted from one another.*

Challenge Number 1 equals the difference between your *month* of birth and your *day* of birth.

Challenge Number 2 equals the difference between your *day* of birth and your *year* of birth.

Challenge Number 3 equals the difference between the *1st challenge number* and the *2nd challenge number*.

Challenge Number 4 equals the difference between your *month* of birth and your *year of birth*.

Remember that all figure work is *subtracted* for finding the challenge numbers.

Before we go any further, let us find Claudia's four challenge numbers, hers are a 0, 2, 2, 2. You can check your own work step by step by following the example, but your numbers will probably be different from Claudia's. These and the reward (pinnacle) numbers can be a little tricky.

Claudia's birthday is November 11, 1966. Her Life path number is an 8.

Her challenge number 1 (a 0) is the difference between her month – November, the 11th month, reduced to a number 2, and her date, also an 11 reduced to a 2. Then 2 - 2 = a zero. A zero can only happen in the 1st challenge when the month and day digits are the same, resulting in a zero when subtracted. Zeros are quite common.

Her challenge number 2 (a 2) is the difference between her day – the 11th reduced to a 2, and her year of birth, a 22 reduced to a 4. 4 - 2 = 2.

Challenge number 3 (a 2) is the difference between the 1st and 2nd challenge numbers. 2 - 0 (zero) = 2.

Challenge number 4 (also a 2) is the difference between her month the 11th reduced to a 2, and her year, a 22 reduced to a 4. 4 - 2 = 2.

Sometimes the challenges are repeated, others can have challenge numbers anywhere from zero through to number 8.

For Claudia, the first challenge of Zero affected her life from her early days through to about her late 20s. The remaining challenges, all number 2s, will be felt throughout the rest of her life until her death and she will learn her various experiences from this number.

Did you manage to get your challenge numbers sorted out and written up?

Now, on to the next stage, the timing of these periods.

The 1st challenge begins at birth.
To find when it will end, you subtract your life path number from 36.

Claudia's life path number is an 8. 36 - 8 = 28. Her 1st challenge, the zero, ends around her 28th birthday and the next challenge takes over around her 29th birthday.

The influences of the future challenges are frequently felt a couple of years before they actually take over.

The 2nd challenge is in effect for the next 9 years. Add 9 to whatever year you have come up with from your previous subtraction.

We add 9 years to Claudia's 29th birthday. 29 + 9 = 38. The 2nd challenge, a number 2 ends around Claudia's 38th birthday.

The 3rd challenge is in effect for a further 9 years. So add another 9 years to the figure you come with.

We add another 9 years to Claudia's 39th birthday. 39 + 9 = 48. This 3rd challenge, also a number 2, ends around Claudia's 48th birthday. From her 49th year, the challenge number 2 will continue for the rest of her life.

The 4th challenge, whatever your number is, continues on until death takes over.

For Claudia, the number 2 will continue to affect her for the rest of her life, both the negative and positive principles of that number. For her, she has been experiencing the energy patterns of the number 2 since she was 29 years old. Obviously she had, and still has, quite a few lessons to learn from that number. If you recall, the number 2 is missing from her chart; it is also one of the weak links in her Christian name. Her balance number, from which she can get help and relief from its positive aspects, is the same number.

You too may have repeating numbers to deal with or each one could be different offering a variety of experiences.

Below are the experiences of each challenge number.

Challenge Number 0

Learning to analyze situations, make choices and act on them for the greatest satisfaction all round is one of the lessons of the zero challenge. You can either give too much or too little of yourself and your resources; therefore, the universe demands you learn to balance.

As there is no number 9 in the challenges, the energies of the zero and 9 are intertwined. Here we usually have a spiritually inclined person who has previously had experiences of the other numbers. Whether the discipline and dedication of walking the Path of Enlightenment is applied in this incarnation is another matter. Nevertheless, there will still be challenges to overcome through the influences of the human race infiltrating your own energy patterns. Your other challenge numbers will direct your attention to working comfortably with them at different stages in your life.

For you, difficulties often appear to be coming from all directions all at the same time, leaving you wondering how to cope with them. This is where analysis and choices spring into action – providing you have developed this necessary ability. This is how you will overcome the obstacles that periodically appear in your life, eventually leading you on to success, happiness, and equanimity.

Challenge Number 1

People in authority tend to oppose you when this challenge enters your life. Learning to deal with this in an even-tempered manner is part of dealing with this challenge. You will keep running into these types of people who leave you with feelings of total frustration. Don't give in. Stand up for yourself, be independent, not giving in to somebody else's demands when you know they are in the wrong. Trust your own judgment.

If challenge number 1 comes up for you at birth through to your mid twenties, it will be parents, family, and teachers who will tend to dominate you. Not much you can do about those early years; hopefully you will not be too cowed by their insistence on doing things their way, as this can leave you with feelings of insecurity and dependency.

Later, in fact, as soon as possible, you should acquire as much self reliance as you can, learn to solve your own problems your own way, develop a sense of identity and refuse to be dominated. As you grow and learn, be careful not to dominate others, becoming opinionated and bossy, as this will be an unconscious habit pattern learned from your elders.

Much trial and error will be experienced during this growth pattern. Of course you will reach "explosion" points in your frustration when you feel you have reached the end of your tether. This is only natural. Part of this challenge is to learn to control your temper without feeling bitter, resentful, or putting the blame onto other people. In fact, putting the blame on somebody else reveals the immaturity of your character. How you feel about what you are experiencing is due to your own emotional reaction – the less you react, the less it can touch you.

It may seem that your dreams and ambitions are continually thwarted by people and circumstances. Stay true to yourself and your dreams of the future. Your other numbers will point the way to your self development. Be aware that pride, ego, impatience, or bossiness could stand in the way of your advancement – these are the lessons and experiences that the number 1 hands you.

Challenge Number 2

Your challenge is recognizing your over sensitivity, self centeredness, self indulgence, and dependence on other people. You tend to sit back, relying on other people, hoping for love, partnership, or a lifetime companion. You must realize that the universe doesn't owe you a living, you have to learn to pull your weight. Your lesson is learning to be independent, to develop your talents, and to share them with the rest of the world. You feel you need attention and approval from others but how are you going to go about getting it?

Your emotional self is always on a roller coaster. When you allow your feelings and emotions to take control of your life, you end up with uncertainties and little self confidence. You fear all sorts of unnecessary things, you read all sorts of meanings into other people's words bringing on emotional turmoil for yourself, then becoming petulant and childish.

Number 2s indeed have some challenges to handle including distressful relationships and addictions, not only drugs or drink, but they convince themselves of all sorts of physical problems and run from doctor to doctor demanding attention. The fascinating thing about this addiction problem is that number 2 seems to be unable or unwilling to recognize that they have this health addiction, yet when they reach a stage of maturity – mid life, and challenge number 3 moves in, quite a few go back to school to take addiction counseling courses to teach others to overcome them!

The challenge this number brings is to learn to see the positive side of yourself and your talents. You have an acute awareness and a strong intuition. You have a great deal of understanding and compassion hidden under that blanket of self centeredness. You also have a tremendous empathy for the inner turmoil that other people are going through, but you are so busy with your own, that you fail to use it.

If you can take all this to heart – without reading other meanings into my words – you can turn yourself around into a positive thinking person who is very capable of using the enormous inner strength and power to overcome difficult situations, not only for yourself but for other people as well. This is what this particular challenge is all about – putting your emotions to one side and handling them in a mature fashion, looking inside yourself to see the diplomatic skills you possess, your talent for organization, and creating harmony amongst groups. As you gradually learn and overcome these challenges, you will find a career that satisfies your needs; your relationships will turn around, bringing you happiness and love. Any addictions you have brought on yourself may well vanish into limbo; then you will be in a position to counsel others who have addiction problems. Having overcome your emotional problems, or some of them, in dealing with this challenging number, you will receive the approval you so desperately seek.

Challenge Number 3

During the time when challenge number 3 is in operation you may find it difficult to express yourself either creatively or individually. The trouble is you are doubting yourself, showing yourself to others on a superficial level, wondering how they will judge you if you show yourself in your true independent, imaginative, and creative self. Does it really matter what people think of you? No two assessments will be the same and all you are doing is bringing anxiety on yourself.

There are many aspects hidden within the numbers. When a challenge comes up, it attacks us on a psychological level. We become aware of things, people, relationships, environments, life in general, and many things we haven't noticed before. We absorb all these energies which now seem to be different, apply them to ourselves in either a positive or negative fashion.

Challenge number 3 suggests you may be assessing yourself from a weak point of view, scattering your energies and talents ending up with a whole stretch of boredom. Do you really want to sit around and twiddle your thumbs for nine years, just gossiping your life away, exaggerating on it yet accomplishing nothing?

You may feel reclusive, lonely, avoiding using any talents you have. Your defenses are up, friends and social activities do not appeal to you any longer. What is wrong? Have you looked around and decided other people are more accomplished than you? Perhaps the lifestyle of your friends seems better than yours and you think you could never reach that standard. These are things you haven't noticed before; they didn't affect you then, so why should you allow them to do so now that you are aware of them. There will be other stuff that comes to your awareness. Don't criticize yourself; recognize you are having a psychological attack – we all have them at various times when we denigrate ourselves. Take stock of yourself and the achievements you have already attained. Think about something you've always wanted to do and never had time to do it; then get on with it.

This challenge often comes at your mid-life term. This can herald a change of career, residence, country, relationship, or a whole complete life style. Your whole thinking patterns are different. If this challenge comes to you at this time of your life, read the different aspects of the number 3 you will find throughout the book and apply the creative portions to yourself. You may even come across an attractive idea within the words that triggers an interest in you, resulting in a talent you weren't aware of, propelling you into a whole new life style.

Challenge Number 4

This number is always a tough one to handle; it literally screams: "Watch out; here come barrow loads of tasks and restrictions." This number is called the taskmaster. I can vouch for that. Number 4 represents my last three challenges and I have had them dropped on me one way or another since my mid twenties. My last challenge of the number 4 continues on until my death. Now I am a widow, on my own with no family to tell me how to run my life, make demands on me, or get me to finish what they started – I can choose my own tasks and the responsibilities that go with them. To compensate this last challenge I have a number 1 reward. Number 1 represents self, independence, initiative, and willpower. Number 1s don't usually get much support from family, which fits nicely into my life framework as I do not have any. I can bring my ideas to the surface regarding which book I shall write next, then get my creativity on the move when I feel like it, without interference from anybody. I can structure my life (number 4) now however I please within the boundaries of the number 4. I share this bit of my life with you to show how the numbers work together, and of course, you have seen how the numbers have fit into Claudia's life with the little capsules I have written previously.

With this number 4 challenge exercising its influence, you will have to learn the lessons of organization and practicality that this challenge brings. It's no good fantasizing about all the lovely things you imagine you can do while ignoring your mundane responsibilities, forgetting to finish things, living in a disorderly fashion that frustrates other people.

You may have difficulty finding work that appeals to you because of a lack of education. Maybe financial circumstances curtailed your schooling, but if there is something in life that you really want to achieve, you will arrange your obligations, discipline yourself, and head for the dream you hold inside.

If life is really so much against you and you are fighting your way through with jobs you do not care for with no way out, this challenge suggests you learn and use patience, understanding, and practical commonsense in your everyday affairs. Number 4 is difficult to handle but if you become headstrong and antagonistic, rebelling against certain responsibilities, people will turn against you. On the other hand, try not to take on everybody's chores, making them feel you are invading and controlling their lives. It's quite a balancing act that is required of you.

The one nice thing about the number 4 challenge is that developing discipline and practicality teaches you to control any overriding emotions that could get in the way of your harmony. Remember number 4 does let up every now and again when the rewards come. You can enjoy this rewarding time before the next onslaught and remember it while you are handling the next set of problems.

Challenge Number 5

Impulsive action is usually the problem here, the challenge being to learn discipline, control, and thinking before taking action. A number 5 represents freedom at any cost. When this challenge enters your life you will find yourself doing many things without considering the consequences because you have such a desire for change and more change. Change is fine as long as you are not running away from responsibilities, so make your changes in an intelligent way.

If the number 5 has come up as your first challenge it could be that your family was always on the move for one reason or another, so your education may be incomplete. This too, could be a cause for job hopping, impulsively moving from one to another that gains you the reputation of being unstable. If you have come from a "movable" family, the other side of the 5 could impress itself on you. You want to stay in one place bypassing certain experiences that the 5 has for you. This constant moving has set up a psychological fear of change, so you tend to hang on to people and situations which really demand change for your own growth. You have become too cautious and non progressive. Flexibility is another lesson of the 5 challenge. Consulting your balance number and working with this challenge number at the same time could be of great benefit.

What you really need during any of the nine year cycles of challenge periods – 2, 3, or 4 – is to have a career where every day is different, bringing interesting facts of life to the public. This will give you a tremendous sense of freedom; your talents and abilities will blossom from which you will gain total fulfillment.

Challenge Number 6

When the number 6 challenge appears in your life you become more aware of your emotional desire to involve yourself with family and close friends. Here you must be very careful that you do not start to control the lives of others. If you set too high a standard or try to become a perfectionist, you will be seen as controlling and demanding and your relationships will dwindle away to nothing. During this time you will learn to walk the tightrope of help and interference and retain your balance.

The number 6 challenge frequently seems to bring on a feeling of dissatisfaction, not only with what you do but with what other people do as well. At this stage, you are likely to ignore your obligations, feel you can't be bothered to keep appointments, becoming self seeking and disorganized. You appear not to be grateful for anything and you have forgotten how to say "thank you." Wrapped up in your own rigid thinking, you are missing out on the beauty of life and yet, in normal circumstances (with other numbers) you are impressed with beauty in all its forms.

The number 6 teaches you to have a balanced perspective regarding the service you provide for others when they need it and your own personal transformation and inner development.

Challenge Number 7

What a dichotomy when challenge number 7 enters your life. Do you rush into spiritual matters believing everything you hear or are you so skeptical that you sneer saying "prove it to me"? Guess what! Challenge number 7 says now it's time for you to investigate and find your own personal philosophy and seek out the purpose of your life. During this 9-year period, you will think intellectually and rationally on the one hand, yet you will be drawn to seeking inside yourself at the same time, but you are not sure what you are looking for. If you are feeling a sense of separation, you may wish to join a group who is also investigating their inner selves, finding different perspectives with which they can cope with life's anomalies. Thoughts, emotions, insight, and love are part of a discussion group that can set your inner self to freedom.

You will have to have faith in this invisible world that makes up the energies that we utilize and respond to each moment. Put your pride, skepticism, complaints, and criticisms to one side; let your feelings run free, which is what this challenge is all about. As you drop these negativities to one side, you may experience an incident from the past that has been holding you back and repressing your feelings of expression and love. Release will come along and remove any suppressed hurt, anger, or grief that you have been carrying around for a life time. Challenge number 7 always does its spiritual work of upliftment, bringing a sense of joy and wonder back into your life as if you are once again a small child of the universe.

Challenge Number 8

This is quite a spiritual test that you will have to endure. Whether it is for a single 9-year cycle or longer depends on your numbers. Whatever length of time you have to experience this challenge, it is dealing with the balance between material wealth, greed, and spiritual well being.

During this period you will find yourself being quite concerned about accumulating money, continually asking yourself, "Will this be enough for my needs?" pushing yourself to get more and more. Status and power also creeps into your thoughts, taking over your life to the exclusion of everything else.

The test of this challenge is to understand that greed can take over bringing out unscrupulous business practices and being ruthless with rivals and subordinates.

Petty jealousies, over indulgence, and wasted effort are the negative side of the number 8 that can cause your downfall leaving you feeling powerless, not knowing which way to go next. Number 8 demands good honest business practices balanced by home life and friendships without taking advantage of anybody else.

You can achieve everything that you want by moving along steadily, step by step, sharing what you have, lending a hand to the needy or being part of your community. This challenge points out that if you are aware of what you need and require and the needs and requirements of others the universe will make sure that you always have exactly what you need.

We are normally utilizing the numbers 1 to 9, but there is no number 9 in the Challenges. The subtractions make it impossible, so the zero takes its place operating on the characteristics of the number 9.

Having understood how the challenges have guided us to take charge of our weaknesses, and transformed as many as we can into strengths, we can move forward into the next chapter and savor the delights of our rewards.

Chapter 9

The Cycles of Rewards

When the cycles of the rewards come around we experience a change of pace and a change of direction. We feel stimulated by the opportunities that come our way even though they bring demands with them. They point out our special attributes that should be applied to our lifestyle for improvement, growth, and attainment. These cycles bring on major changes. Each of the 4 cycles of rewards bring with it a number whose qualities indicate a time and type of personal experience and transformation. Each cycle is a period of further development utilizing the lesson and experience learned from the previous challenge. If you failed that particular test, your rewards at this time will be rather mediocre instead of sparkling and stimulating.

Just like the challenges, the energies of each reward period lasts nine years, running concurrently with the challenges, but the reward numbers will be different from the challenge numbers even though they work in tandem. The challenge number shows you the weakness you need to tackle and the reward number shows you how to go about it and what you can accomplish.

Once again we need to use the full birth data. This time we will *add* the figures as opposed to the subtraction we used in defining the challenges. We shall arrive at the numbers first, but you will find the timing exactly the same as the challenges because they work hand in hand. All the numbers *except 11 and 22* should be reduced to a single digit. With the reward cycle we use these powerful numbers.

To find the 1st reward add the numbers of your month and day of birth.

As usual I will use Claudia's birth date as an example.

November (11th month) 11th day, 1966 year (22). 11th month + 11th day = 22. 22 is her first reward number.

To find the 2nd reward add the day of your birth to the year of your birth.

Claudia: day 11 + year 22 = 33 = 6. Her 2nd reward number is 6.

To find the 3rd reward: add the 1st reward number to the 2nd.

Claudia: 22 + 6 = 28 = 10 = 1. Her 3rd reward number is 1.

To find the 4th reward number: add the month of birth to the year of birth.

Claudia: month 11 + 22 year = 33 = 6. Her 4th reward number is a number 6 again.

Throughout Claudia's first 28 years, she was coping with a 0 (zero) challenge plus the strong energies of the reward number 22. Her very early years would have had little *awareness* impact on her but as she grew up, her dreams of creating something big for the rest of the world to see, use, and enjoy lay snugly within her desire world. She kept this vision to herself knowing that time would take care of it.

An interesting fact here. If you reduce the letters of the word *time* to numbers you will see that they come to an 11 – one of Claudia's master numbers, which would eventually have an impact on her for the rest of her life. Time also made its impact; it was a lesson she had to learn in understanding it, and controlling it, the empty number 7 in her third triangle.

Her Zero challenge number indicates her deep spirituality, which hadn't yet surfaced, but her inner self knew that her desire would be fulfilled at a later date when friends and supporters would be there to give help. This actually started to happen a few years before her 2nd challenge (a number 2) and her reward (a number 6) took place.

If you look at Claudia's chart, Figure 1A, you will see the master numbers of her birth being used as 2s and 4s, the weaker side of the numbers; she was also allowing the energies of the number 6 of her name to be imposed on her by family demands. (The number 8 of her Life Path had yet to come into power, which it did when she reached her 30s).

In 1986, just before her 20th birthday arrived, she was about to move into a number 1 personal year (more in the next chapter). With the number 9 year she was just moving out of, she got up her courage (number 1) to become her own self, do what she wanted to do. She took the plunge, shucked off the restrictions (number 6), and got more in touch with herself. She dealt with the stresses, problems, obstacles, and oppositions that stood in her way of moving forward. At the end of the number 9 cycle she felt relieved, as if she was on the breakthrough of a new positive life style. And so she was. This was the time of the start of her art career and when she met her future husband.

Here are the Reward Interpretations that take place at the same times of the Challenges.

Number 1

You are being offered independence, growth, and self improvement, if you have the courage to bounce back from the previous challenge and its difficult experiences.

To which reward period does this number apply? If it is applying to the first period, it is asking you to develop your strength of character and establish your individuality in readiness for the challenges of the mundane world at a later date.

In your youth, original ideas began to form; you began to recognize you had leadership abilities, which could have produced self-centeredness, stubbornness, or egotistical traits. If you developed these, your challenge number will catch up with you sometime in life and you will have the opportunity to control or remove them.

In the second and third periods, you can develop your talents. You will know your own strengths and capabilities sufficient to put your unconventional ideas into action, turn them into reality, and bring them before the public, if this is your desire.

In the fourth period, the latter stage of your life you will keep going with no particular desire to completely retire. You will still have challenges to cope with that will bring changes once more into your life. No doubt you will embrace these and continue to develop your ideas and talents that are still waiting in the background of your life.

Number 2

If this number was in operation during the first years of your life you were likely to be an over-sensitive child. This would be one of your challenges that you would need to overcome or it would prove to be detrimental to your later achievements. Your mother may have been a strong influence during this time, quite possibly squashing your verbal and emotional expression leaving you with later difficulties.

The productivity of the second and third period will depend on your ability to work patiently and willingly with others, developing your self confidence and facing your short comings. By using your insight and understanding you will obtain a great deal of appreciation but being forceful or confrontational will only work against you.

By the time the fourth period comes along, in the latter part of your life you should have developed patience, tact, and diplomacy, which is part of your life's work. Harmony and peace will have been achieved whether you continue to work or just retire gracefully.

Number 3

The 9-year reward cycle of the number 3 brings a great deal of enjoyable activities. It's also a very creative time to expose any of your talents and abilities. During this time you could be involved with friends, entertainment, travel, or social affairs.

If this number comes up on your first period you will tend to be rather scattered in your childhood with so much creative and artistic potential, but not knowing what to do with it. Unless you have guidance from parents or teachers in your youth, you may not have worked hard enough to develop them. This means that when opportunities come at a later date, you will either not recognize them or have to let them go because you do not have the ability to handle them.

When the second and third periods come along there will be opportunities for writing, speaking, design work, anything in the creative or entertainment field that appeals to you or that you have been training for. Travel is also on the agenda. This is the time when you should be taking on the responsibilities of your life, putting your finances in order and making ready for your later retirement. Because things are going so well for you, there is a tendency to drift along, but this should be nipped in the bud.

When the fourth period comes along, provided you have made your mark during the previous period, you should be able to comfortably enjoy the social field, travel, and to live in relative comfort in this retirement time. If you have developed your writing or designing or any other form of expression that you can do at home, you do not need to fully retire until you or death makes the decision.

Number 4

The number 4 period denotes a practical and realistic approach to life, developing order and organization. Over this 9-year cycle, hard work comes your way whether you want it or not and you will finally build the determination and effort to handle it.

If you experience this number in the first period of your life you can look back and see that a lot of your youthful activities were curtailed for various reasons. There could be two reasons, one being the necessity to join the workforce at an early age to help with family finances, or you just didn't want to continue with your education; or secondly, because you have chosen to further your education, and study is your choice rather than the social atmosphere as you are steadily building for your future.

Benefits will come to you during the second and third periods particularly if it was your education you were previously following. This will enable you to get ahead of the competition and achieve whatever you have set out to obtain.

During the fourth period, heading towards retirement days, there will be very little desire to slow down and relax. You feel the need to constantly have a sense of accomplishment, to be busy with something that brings you pleasure and satisfaction. There are of course, the unfortunate ones whose pleasure of retirement will be curtailed due to economic restrictions.

Number 5

Freedom and getting rid of responsibilities is the aura of the 5 cycle. Change can suddenly appear in your life, friends come and go, there will be more variety in your working atmosphere and in your leisure activities. Your finances will rapidly change as well, going up and down so you had better think about building a nest egg for your later retirement.

If number 5 comes up as your first period this can be difficult for you in your childhood. Change always seems to be on the horizon for some reason or another requiring you to change schools, friends, and the social atmosphere. This is usually unsettling for children and it may have some psychological effect later in life.

In the second and third periods, the ability to take a changeable environment in your stride will be to your advantage, giving you the sense of freedom you desire. You will feel the need for travel and adventure. Look for a job or career that offers these; look also at your challenge number that's affecting you at this time and work the two together.

Number 5 in the fourth period can bring a most interesting time as you will find change and variety keeping you occupied. If you have salted away money for this particular time of life you will have no worries. You may also find domestic affairs no longer impose themselves on you, giving you the freedom to do whatever you wish and go wherever you feel like going.

Number 6

When number 6 appears in your reward programs, be prepared for restrictions and responsibilities. These usually involve family, children, home affairs, or your environment which imposes itself on you.

In the first period, when you were a young person, you may have had the responsibility of younger members of the family thrust on you. Parents or authority figures place their demands on you leaving you feeling pressured and limited with no time for yourself. You should try to avoid an early marriage for the problems and further restrictions it may bring.

In the second and third periods you will reap your benefits in financial and business matters. People who have the necessary requirements to help you achieve your goals appear on the scene to aid you at the right moment.

A number 6 in the last period sees the satisfaction of your growth and progress throughout your previous years. Looking back, you can see how you have developed yourself in many different areas becoming a loving parent, an excellent business person providing well for family, and becoming an esteemed person in your community.

Number 7

During the time when the 9-year cycle of number 7's influence arrives, you will feel you need times of isolation, being alone to contemplate what life has handed you and what will be the next step to take. This is the time to take stock of your inner resources, to develop them and balance them with material matters and practical affairs.

In the first period during your growing years you are not likely to have many friends – if any at all. You are a loner with different interests from the people surrounding you and you are not easily understood. Growing up is a difficult time, for you do not toe the line as others do. While they are out carousing or playing, you prefer to read poetry or take walks in the country to feel the rhythms of nature, contemplating the forces of the universe. You may be observed as a "gifted" child, in which case your parents may see that your education will be exactly right for you to fit into the world. Your interests are in learning, investigating, research, and gaining skills which will enhance your lifestyle at a later date.

The number 7 in the second and third periods invites research, to become an expert in one particular field, to delve into the philosophical side of life, perhaps investigating the various religions of the world. This is the time to specialize, although it will be a slow time in your life and the financial benefits will not be great.

In the fourth period, the number 7 brings opportunities to share your knowledge with the rest of the world. You have much wisdom, knowledge, and spiritual growth. People will look up to you and admire you for what you will share with them. You will enhance their lives by showing them the understandings of the connection between body, mind, and spirit.

Number 8

This number is asking for the balance between the material world and the spiritual. It brings business and moral responsibilities; it is a time of material growth, expansion, and reward. Your personal power shows through your sound judgment, organizational and management procedures. You are very capable of handling large enterprises and the problems they produce, yet you enjoy handling them because you like a challenge.

Number 8 in the first period indicates an ambitious child who is likely to get into business or commerce at an early age. Being a practical thinker, this child will have money, success, and status at the top of his/her priorities.

In the second and third periods, opportunities to reach executive status will be opened due to rational thinking and approach and the spiritual recognition of the needs of others.

In the last period, business affairs and the high position attained will put retirement very firmly on a back burner. Many, many 8s are surrounded by an atmosphere of status and power and are reluctant to give up this position until illness or death calls.

Number 9

In total contrast to the number 8s material approach to life, number 9 is the humanitarian who has great concern for the weaker, poorer, unfortunate folk who have little power to help themselves. This philanthropic attitude is wrapped up in emotionalism which sometimes can go overboard not knowing when they are being "conned." You need to make a balance between the needs of others and your own personal requirements. You must not become a selfless martyr.

Number 9 in the first period of life is often the child who befriends an unpopular child who is being bullied. Even at an early stage this child will feel a sense of social responsibility and compassion starting off by giving away favorite toys to those who have little or none.

In the second and third period you may be drawn towards travel to less fortunate countries where help and understanding is required. This is also a time when there is growth in financial and business affairs but it will be accompanied by a large challenge at the same time. If you have a strong artistic or creative streak in you, this talent will be brought to the surface and you will feel the need to utilize it. If you happen to be a dedicated business person this creative streak will show itself through becoming a patron of the arts or a benefactor supporting theater productions or art schools.

During the fourth period, you are likely to become more philanthropic, caring more about people and the misfortunes of the rest of the world. If you have been lucky enough to amass a fortune or large sums of money you will donate freely to worthy causes thereby balancing your spiritual life with your fortunate material times.

Number 11

This is the first of the master numbers offering tremendous spiritual and personal growth, yet at the same time you will experience great demands on you, both emotional and spiritual. You will feel yourself enmeshed in spiritual forces, your sensitivity is heightened and your awareness opens giving you experiences that you have never had before. This will bring on some nervous tension as you are not quite sure how to handle the changes that are going on within you. At this time you must become as practical as you possibly can even though you may feel as if you are different from other people. No doubt you are if you have absorbed metaphysical disciplines and spiritual energies. All you can do about that is to use your creative and unconventional approach to problems, do what you can to be of help and service where it is needed, trust your intuition, keep your feet on the ground, and find places of quiet and beauty that will restore your inner peace.

If number 11 is operating as the first reward young people will not be aware of the spiritual forces being beamed at them. They are more likely to be responding to the impulses of the number 2 (that's 1 + 1 of the 11) being very cooperative and a friend to everybody. At this early stage of life, companionship is very necessary; you need outlets for your emotions and creativity. If you are close to your mother, you can gain great benefit from her understanding and love.

In the second and third periods, there will be little difference between these and the first period except responsibilities will come your way through going off to university with extensive studies or joining the workforce, where you will be inspired to reach out for particular accomplishments.

During the 4th period, this latter part of your life will bring you the opportunities to share your inspirational knowledge that you have been collecting all your life. You will be guided towards some particular work or outlet for release of this very special spiritual force through which you will receive great rewards.

Number 22

This is the second of the master numbers demanding efficiency and the determination to bring your dreams and plans from the archetypal world that you have visualized to fruition in the material world. You need to be practical to build your structure, whatever it is; courage is needed to share your dream. Have faith, for you have many friends and supporters from both worlds – the spiritual and material – which seems to involve either business or government, perhaps both. At this time, you have a vast influence and power which is well recognized.

During the 1st period of life, this master number will have very little influence. Being the master builder, the influences will be more in keeping with number 4 (2+2 of the 22), children being more inclined to build the structure of life from their own viewpoint. What happens during this period sets the tone for the next period.

To handle the second and third periods efficiently and successfully, it is essential that you received the education necessary to handle big business or governmental positions. If so, you are on your way to fulfilling those dreams and visions that you have harbored for years. Without it, you will not have the capacity or the opportunity to bring them to fruition in the way you envision. The number 4 will hold its influence over you instead and you will find yourself working to build structures for other people in the business world or the field of government, always being in the background.

For the final period, the latter stages of life, if you have reached the recognition and status you desired during the previous two periods, you will just keep on going until your body gives up and the angel of death crooks a finger. Otherwise, you will just plod along until retirement time beckons when you can decide what you want to do with your spiritual and material and creative talents.

Now that you know how to work out the times of your Challenge periods (previous chapter) and your Reward numbers from your Life Path number, here's an easy chart to consult covering the years for all the Life Path numbers. The master numbers 11 and 22 have the same time span as the numbers 2 and 4. This chart covers the dates for both the Challenges and the Rewards as they happen at the same time. Just look at your Life Path number and it will tell you the years they are in action. (An additional copy of this chart can be found in the Appendix.)

Putting together your challenge numbers, and your reward numbers, united with your character and personality, you will experience many pleasures and surprises. In fact, every time we have a new challenge and reward, we are offered a different part for us to play on this stage we call life. Sometimes, we can be the star of the show; other times, we just have to be the understudy. It all depends on how we learned our lines and performed at the audition (the challenge).

Let us move along on our journey now and see what the future holds for you in the personal years ahead.

Combination Chart

Life Path #	First Challenge and Reward Age/Years	Second Challenge and Reward Age/Years	Third Challenge and Reward Age/Years	Final Challenge and Reward Age/Years
1	0 to 35	36 to 45	46 to 55	56 to life end
2/11	0 to 34	35 to 44	45 to 54	55 to life end
3	0 to 33	34 to 43	44 to 53	54 to life end
4/22	0 to 32	33 to 42	43 to 52	53 to life end
5	0 to 31	32 to 41	42 to 51	52 to life end
6	0 to 30	31 to 40	41 to 50	51 to life end
7	0 to 29	30 to 39	40 to 49	50 to life end
8	0 to 28	29-38	39 to 48	49 to life end
9	0 to 27	28 to 37	38 to 47	48 to life end

Chapter 10

Your Personal Year Cycle

There are many cycles in life – your name and birth data coming under their dominion. Some are long-term cycles like the Life Path cycles; others are the short-term periods of 9 years like the challenges and rewards, or the 7-year cycles that are the underlying cycles of life and the rhythms of the universe. Each time we go through one of these repeating cycles we learn something new from each of these numbers with their experiences; then we acquire new knowledge and wisdom from each one.

Each reward has brought us the opportunity to expand our knowledge, giving us further growth and the productivity to be applied to our lives. Each challenge number presents us with a specific lesson that needs to be given special attention. It's these two cycles that drive us along the major long-term cycle of our Life Path for us to carry out, or make a good attempt at carrying out, the destiny we have chosen. So our lives are really lived through the wisdom and knowledge we've absorbed over the years and our losses and gains depend on the way we apply what we have acquired.

Your Personal Year cycle is one where you can see the energy patterns of any particular year ahead; prepare for it by adjusting and applying the knowledge you have of yourself to the requirements of that year. Once again, it is a 9-year cycle (1-9), and each number that you will experience has its own characteristics bringing different stages of development for you.

At the same time that you are influenced by your personal year, our planet also has its own year of influence that everybody in the world relates to. This is called the Universal year. As each new year begins, the universal year has progressed to a different number, just as each of your birthdays bring a new personal year number for you.

These numbers are easy to calculate, but we need to do the universal year first because this is always added to your birth month and day to get the answer for your personal year.

To find the universal year number, add together the 4 digits of any particular year you require. For instance, to arrive at the universal year for 1988, add all the numbers together: 1 + 9 + 8 + 8 = 26 = 8. So the universal year number for 1988 is an 8. Its influence on the minds and emotions of the members of the human race were making money – with a capital M. There was an all-out effort in business, banks, stock markets, multi corporations, all money-making operations plus governments and political organizations to rake in as much profit as possible. Many people were inclined to start their own businesses and small businesses and owner operators were thinking about expanding. That's part of the way the number 8 universal year operates.

Now, to find your own personal year number so that you know what is going to happen to you during the year you have selected you *add* together the *month and day of your birth plus* the universal year number of your choice. The total of these three is your personal year number starting from your birthday of that year to your next birthday when it will move into the next number. There seems to be quite a bit of confusion amongst numerologists as to whether the personal year starts in January with the start of the universal year or whether it actually starts on the person's birthday. I favor the personal year starting on the birthday, after all, it is *your* personal day of birth and it seems to work very well for all my students.

Anyway, back to Claudia as our example, using a past year to interpret.

> We know that 1988 is a universal number 8 year. Claudia's birth month is November, the 11th month, and her day of birth is also an 11. We add 11 + 11 + 8 (the universal year) = 30 = 3. Claudia's personal year number starting from her birthday on November 11, 1988 will be a creative number 3. But, now follow carefully, from her previous birthday in November 1987. She had just started operating under a number 2 personal year in the latter part of a number 7 universal year. (January 1987 adds up to 25 = 7.) When the year changed over on January 1, 1988 to a number 8 universal year, Claudia would continue on under the influence of her number 2 *personal* year until her birthday in November 1988 (when the number 3 would take over) yet the energies of the universal year number 8 were already imposing themselves on her inner self giving her some thoughts of business.

I hope I have made this bit clear as it can be difficult to understand for people whose birthdays come near to the closing months of the year; they are always lagging behind the influences. But unless you have a birthday on January 1st or close by the influences of the universal year would always be ahead of your personal year.

Another thing about the energy patterns of the numbers of your personal year, I find they invariably start to bring their pressure to bear just a few months before the actual birthday. The old energies are on their way out and the new ones are pushing their way in so you will likely find a mixture of the two. My personal year starts in July and I always find the new energies infiltrating myself round about mid April or the beginning of May.

Continuing with the theme of Claudia's personal year, as she voiced her thoughts and intentions of developing her business, she gained a lot of cooperation (the number 2) from her new husband whom she married in 1987, (her personal number 2 year), his family and her family encouraging her in arranging a disciplined schedule for herself (recall she is missing the number 7 in her chart) becoming aware of time, designing the art work for her creations, working out the details and problems and honing her skills for her personal number 3 year to start. Not only that, there was the structure of the relationship she and Cody were very nicely building together. With help and guidance, she did all the advertising and all the necessary bits to start her business a few months before her birthday in November, then launched everything for the Christmas sales. Perfect timing and it was very successful. This was all in keeping with the universal year number 8 being the same number as Claudia's life path number 8. It was a most auspicious year for her as part of her destiny came to fruition.

Personal Year Interpretations

Year Number 1

This is the year when you begin a new cycle, a whole new adventure of challenges and rewards during this 9-year cycle.

It will be easier to assert yourself this year and your initiative and leadership will receive cooperation from many people. The cosmic forces are on your side so take advantage of them. Major projects begun will continue along with the extra responsibilities they will bring. New business opportunities will present themselves and new contacts made during this number 1 year are usually more worthwhile than at other times. Choose your partnerships and friends with care, then they will likely stay with you for the next nine years.

Steps taken in a 1 year should be considered more carefully than usual and the specter of over optimism studiously banished. The intensity of this tide will carry you forward, so be careful that you do not become sloppy on details or make impossible promises because the tides that you have set in motion may sweep you under. Avoid vacillation, jumping to premature conclusions and self doubts along with bluffing and sneaky tactics and you will gain benefit. Bear in mind that everything you do now will affect your future.

Your mental outlook is important this year as your creative and inventive powers are at their peak. Concentrate on producing results. Study, write, find creative arts, new business ideas – put your dreams in motion. Naturally, you will find strong opposers to your chosen path during this number 1 year, so be prepared to face any "strong-arm" methods with a strength of your own.

It can be a pioneering year for you; promote yourself and your ideas, be ready for major changes. You should have interesting and stimulating experiences now that you have shucked off unwanted stuff from the previous year of number 9 and closed off that nine year cycle.

Welcome in the change and all that goes with it. Willpower and self discipline will lead you to prestige and profit. This is a marvelous time; use it to full advantage.

Year Number 2

This is the year when you will build the relationships that you started in the previous year. Partnerships can develop, grow, and expand, and what was planted in the previous year – either positive or negative – begins to sprout. This is the law of seedling growth and development time so you may find yourself more in the background this year, slowing down compared to last year, working on self improvement and acquiring skills and knowledge. Work on the minor aspects of your life rather than taking on any new projects. Problems and details should be taken care of immediately as they appear.

This is a year to learn patience, cooperation, giving a helping hand; it is a year of self control especially where your emotions are concerned, as they can be blown out of proportion and exaggerated. If you are feeling sad, you will tend towards despair, while happiness goes in the other direction with feelings of ecstasy. Older people and parents may try your patience; keep calm and recognize that this is a challenge to be handled as well as a chance to develop your tact and diplomacy.

Deep relationships, including marriage, can occur within a number 2 year, for married people a deepening of feelings will be experienced. Watch out for deceit within the home life. If you are in a bad relationship, divorce or separation can now take place. Aggressiveness and impatience will cause many problems.

Year Number 3

This is the happy year, a time of fruition or success but you can also fritter away your harvest whether it is money or talents. If you live high on the hog now, you will pay the consequences later; better to keep your goals in mind, expand your creative talents, particularly those relating to writing, speaking, selling. If a sale has been hanging fire, it will be completed in this number 3 year. If business sales have been slow, more success is likely now. This is an excellent year to present your ideas or schemes to influential people as your personality is quite expansive. It is an excellent selling cycle, a time when you can get rid of unneeded household or personal items at better than average prices.

Self expression is high on the list for a number 3 year, especially the written word, whether it is a story, a play, a script, a proposal, or an idea. Be careful with your words, examine any documents or agreements carefully before signing. Anything that brings you into the public eye will bring you success, especially where radio, TV, or platform appearances are concerned.

Do remember that you need discipline and focus to achieve any of these successes and the number 3 year will tempt you in the opposite direction of over indulgence and frivolity. Social relationships will be high on your list;

you will entertain and be entertained, friends will help you spend your money especially in the area of travel, pleasure, and meeting exciting people.

Love is in the air, a new romance, a marriage or perhaps a "honeymoon" without the ties.

This cycle is for your enjoyment and also for your success. Balance is the keyword so make the most of it.

Year Number 4

Responsibility is the keyword for a number 4 year. You need to be organized and practical, yet flexible enough to recognize and use any of the opportunities that will come your way. Your discipline, concentration, and focus should be in place this year, an improvement over last year! Next year will be a year of many changes so it is best that you get a firm foundation in place this year. Don't try to expand in a number 4 year; you will hit above average snags and difficulties. Concentrate on your existing material affairs and they will prosper, even though you may feel overweighted with responsibilities.

Take stock of your assets during this year and improve your business methods. Cement existing partnerships and friendships that can bring you later benefit. Right now, in this 4 year, you are building a solid foundation for security in the years to come through your connections and accomplishments. This is a year of frustration, hard work, and effort and you will feel overburdened and not able to see the results you desire even though they are there. You tend to have your blinkers on. Changing direction is futile, changing employment is ill advised, if it can possibly be avoided.

The lamp of your personality, charm, and magnetism is burning low right now and your physical energy may also be at a low level. When you feel like this, rest up when you can and think of the good times that are ahead of you in the coming years.

Romance and emotional matters are also going to take a back seat during this year, taking second place to material matters which must be dealt with, but it is a good time for balancing family relationships . Time for recreation is also in short supply. Never mind, deal with all your affairs and make ready for the hectic and stimulating year that is just ahead.

Year Number 5

Are you ready for changes, surprises, and new opportunities? They are going to come whether you want them or not. If you have any despondency left over from the grueling 4 year, throw it overboard and move forward. Turning points in your destiny often occur with a number 5 year. Be prepared. This is the year to throw off the old from last year, bring in new methods, promote yourself, seek out people, follow your social and friendly impulses. Go places, do things, and reap some of the rewards of the work done in the previous cycles.

Similar to the number 3, words have greater power than normal. Lecturing, teaching, writing, dramatics, radio, TV, all communications including self advertising are favorably aspected.

If you are intellectually inclined, you will gain great pleasure from study, reading, theatre, music – this is a time for self enjoyment.

Don't plan too far ahead in this number 5 year. Travel for business or pleasure could suddenly come into your life, and if you've made a rigid schedule you might have to miss out on this pleasure. Don't sign long leases or agreements; they will only have to be renegotiated later due to a change of circumstances. You will notice that changes made during this year often undergo further changes fairly soon; it's an unpredictable year. If you think you've found your dream or retirement home during this year, be advised that it will not be with you for too long no matter how much you believe it at the time.

Your sex appeal is in fine shape, but romance in a 5 year is not often harmonious. Sexual experiments will give temporary excitement but not much lasting satisfaction.

Avoid new partnerships if you can or branch out to be your own boss. These are most likely to come to grief in a 5 year. It's very much a free-wheeling year with major changes affecting your career, family situation, and your residence.

Year Number 6

This number 6 year brings on extra responsibilities for family, loved ones, and close friends. It would seem that some family members will need firm direction from you. If there are any marital problems left over from the previous years, they can be easily solved during these harmonious vibrations. The longing for love and a congenial circle of friends will likely be satisfied this year.

Employment looks good, occupational and financial challenges will be light and easy to handle. Your needs and assets hold a very nice balance throughout this year, so you will be able to spend some on the home, redecorate, buy new furnishings or even purchase a new home. Real estate sales should be good if this is your career.

For others who are in the creative area of performing arts, you can see success during the number 6 year. Educational progress is also favored. Learning a new subject, expanding an existing one, or taking on a home study course, will all be easy in this number 6 year.

You probably won't be able to save much money this year, but balance your budget as you go along. Don't accept verbal promises from anyone regarding business prospects or purchases; these can cause problems, break ups of partnerships, even a marriage. Make sure a written agreement is signed by both parties.

Year Number 7

A number 7 year is mainly one of introspection, contemplation, and gaining some understanding of yourself, but avoid brooding over past wrongs and injustices – they are already over and done with. If you dwell on your past mistakes, they can return to haunt you.

You will be spending some time alone or in activities which require a peaceful and tranquil atmosphere. This is the time to get away from business pressures and outside responsibilities if you can manage it, as your material affairs are likely to slow down during this number 7 year. They cannot be hurried at this time. Your physical energy may also be low during this period. A vacation to a retreat or a lonely place away from crowds would be most beneficial.

Number 7 is most definitely against material expansion, it being under the dominion of mystical vibrations, meditation, and heightened intuition. Avoid speculation, gambling, and investment until next year; meditation and mind work will achieve more than material striving. Sometimes, to bolster your bank balance, a number 7 year brings inheritances, out-of-court settlements, or donations.

During this slow year look towards inspirational, creative pursuits, research or invention, studying or writing. Number 7 is an intellectual number stimulating your mind. If you are at the start of a career, look for one in the travel or communications field where unexpected good fortune may lie.

This can be a very peaceful year for many number 7s, if you can accept the philosophical nature of this number which can bring spiritual enlightenment.

Year Number 8

If you have refreshed yourself with the slow nature of the previous number you should be ready to handle this power year of number 8, where you can make great strides in your life. You will begin to feel ambitious. This is the year when you can make big decisions, achieve your goals. Success in business and financial affairs can arrive much more easily this year with your executive powers coming to the surface. Taking command of situations should be quite simple for you.

You are in the frame of mind now where you can influence powerful people to give you assistance; top executives respond to direct approach. Opportunities for advancement are around you and recognition of the work done in the past is likely to come this year depending on the amount of effort you have put into the previous seven years. The rewards are always in proportion to the amount of effort and motivation you put in. If you haven't put much in during the previous years, expect losses of some kind this year even to the point of bankruptcy and failure. Only you are aware of the expenditure of your energies; you have no one else to blame.

If you have worked within the energy patterns of the previous numbers, the inner strength, confidence and further understanding of yourself you have gained from the soul searching number 7 year, it will carry you through to the height of your ambitions. Number 8 is not a totally "selfish" number. The law of compensation offers you a chance to give aid to others not so fortunate. Within the ethics of share and share alike perhaps you could involve yourself in some charitable work, volunteer part of your time and services to some philanthropic organization.

Having understood your part in the world, expansion should head your list of plans. From this, remuneration arrives from the interests you have been pursuing since your number 1 year.

Year Number 9

We finally reach the end of this 9-year cycle. It's time to close the door on this set of experiences, get rid of the old, worn out and unwanted, both physically and mentally, to make way for the start of another nine year cycle next year. This is the year of completion. All things eventually come to an end, this one signaling the end of one type of living for a different one next year. Look forward to it with enthusiasm as a whole new set of experiences are waiting in the wings for you. With each new 9-year cycle and numbers you go through, you will learn something totally different from the challenges and rewards you will be going through. Now you will you see yourself, the people, and world around you through a totally unique viewpoint.

You will have a variety of experiences in this number 9 year; your psychological attitude towards its vibrations are very important. Old thinking patterns should be revised, wasteful ways recognized and turned around along with destructive habit patterns. If you hang onto them, you will make little or no progress when the number 1 year for the new cycle comes about next year. The old patterns will hold you back setting the tone for the whole next 9-year cycle. It's a fast moving time now when you can force issues out into the open and overcome them.

During this time of elimination you can get rid of hangers-on who are draining you emotionally, mentally, physically, and financially, replacing them with abstracts like happiness, love, and understanding.

This you will find easy to do as your intuition and hunches will start developing at a fast rate. Rely on them; all your psychic powers will open up and be of great value to you during the start of the next cycle where you can confidently rely on your first impressions.

This number 9 is the ruler of occultism. Maybe you find yourself being interested in investigating psychic phenomena; so study it, get involved in the spiritual side of life as well and thoroughly enjoy the winds of change on both the material and spiritual levels of life.

We come to the end of the 9 personal years which you can easily apply to yourself. Further information about your life ahead can be gathered from the Law of 7 Cycles which we will cover in the next chapter.

Chapter 11

The Law of 7 Cycles

Rather than going into the month and day cycles which you can find in any numerological book, I have here a far more useful life-giving cycle of seven divisions. These seven, which fit neatly into each of your years, are more informative than month/day cycles which are only a rather weak adaptation of your personal years. When you apply these 7 cycles along with your personal year, you can make your plans ahead of time with confidence, knowing that it is the right time.

Earlier in the book, I drew your attention to the number 7 being a mysterious and powerful number, complete in itself because of its connection to the inner rhythms of the universe which, incidentally also moves in cycles. Apart from this, the human body goes through complete cycles, physical and mental, every 7 years. Learning and understanding takes place within the first four periods of 7 years (that's 28 years, in line with your life path). When you get to the age of 56, you can see how you've applied your actions and reactions (your karmic choices) to these episodes. Why wait until you are 56 or older to look back and see where you made your errors, jumped to conclusions, and made a wrong decision which brought further consequences for you to deal with?

Every day we are faced with making decisions of some sort whether it is a business proposition, deciding to buy or sell something, build a house, take a journey; there are proper periods that guarantee much greater success and satisfaction because they are in harmony with cosmic law.

Your life path number (your cosmic ray) that energized you at birth continues to direct impulses of its own characteristic nature to you. To these you respond with your thoughts or actions. If the energies of the ray are in an upswing movement, your choice will be successful. In a downswing movement, you've chosen the wrong time, experiencing failure or frustration.

Just as we have these cycles of 7 years, so each year of your life is made up of 7 inner cycles, starting with your birthday, just like your personal year. These 7 cycles are made up of approximately 52 days, each offering different opportunities to be grabbed and used or suggesting a way to solve your problems.

To find your own private cycle you will need a calendar. Start with your birthday and count off 52 days, then mark in your dates on the lines below. Follow that with the next date, counting forward again 52 days for the 2nd period, continuing on until you have dated all 7 cycles. For instance, Claudia, who was born on November 11th would count 52 days from her birth date ending on January 2nd. She would fill in her dates on the lines following for the first cycle from November 11th to January 2nd. She would then count a further 52 days onwards from January 3rd to February 23rd, which she would write alongside her second cycle. Her third cycle would start on the 24th of February and she would continue counting onwards in 52 days until she had dated each of the seven cycles. During each of these dates she can consult the interpretations for the most propitious times to carry out each of her intentions.

Count your own 52 day periods starting from your birthday, then write in the dates at the top of each cycle. (You will find a larger chart to mark your cycles in the Appendix if needed.)

7 Cycles

Cycle	Date
First:	
Second:	
Third:	
Fourth:	
Fifth:	
Sixth:	
Seventh:	

First Cycle

The first 52 days from your birthday is a time of opportunity. Make the most of it by asking favors of people who have either the power or the influence to assist you. Push yourself forward right now, show your integrity, change your job, or seek employment. The time is right.

If you need a bank loan, make the appointment at the bank and build up your credit standing. If you are looking to make an investment, this is the time; the same applies to compromises or adjustments in your business or business relationships.

Promote and advertise your business during these 52 days. Build up sales and goodwill, seek recommendations and support from prominent people who will procure beneficial results. Government officials can be very helpful with contracts of any sort.

Healthwise, your vitality should be at its best during this cycle. If you have arrived at this period feeling a little low, your health will improve rapidly. Pay attention to your eyes and try not to strain them with extra work or reading. If you need to have an operation of any sort, this is the time to let it happen.

Second Cycle

This is a time when changes can be made or things finished up. Important short journeys can be successfully made. It's a time of movement, so don't try to plan any permanent change or start a new career, and above all, don't sign contracts or try to make arrangements for something you would like to last for a long time. They will all fall through. Any verbal agreements you make will either be ignored or changed at a later date.

Changes in employees or their duties can be made successfully along with alterations in business practices. This is a good period to build up your business friendships and to contact new clients or customers.

The most propitious area of business in these 52 days is with companies who deal in movable things – freight, cargoes, trains that carry commercial goods, vehicles that carry liquids, chemicals, gasoline, oil; it is an exceptionally successful time, more than any other. Hotels, restaurants, car rentals, tour buses, cruise lines, and travel agencies should see an increase in business during this period. This is also a good cycle for public speakers and performers who travel from place to place.

Don't borrow or lend money at this time; neither should you speculate in the stock market or any other form of gambling or get involved in a project that requires a good deal of investment. Construction of a new building should not be started; or changes to the plans will need to be made which will prove to be costly.

This cycle brings temporary changes in the physical body, they come and go quickly. You may have a headache or stomach upset, a 24-hour type of flu, pick up a cold, have a minor earache, or your eyes will feel tired. Your mind and emotions will have an impact on your body so don't dwell on any discomfort; you will only make it worse. Rest up, remain optimistic about your affairs, put your mind and attention on other promising things and everything will pass fairly quickly.

Third Cycle

Here you will need discrimination and good judgment to get you through these 52 days. You will have so much energy that you are likely to jump in with both feet without thinking things through carefully, taking on projects that have no possibility of success, or others that will take so long to come to fruition that you will eventually have to abandon them. If you have had problems in the past that are still blocking your progress, this is the time to address them and get them out of the way. At the same time consider those competitors or enemies who get in the way of your success and ways to deal with them amicably without using lawyers or going to court. This is not the greatest period for either sex to deal with women, but it is favorable for women to ask men for assistance or favors in either business or social matters.

Arguments and conflicts will turn out badly right now, but if you are in the selling business and need to convince your purchaser, gentle force will be to your advantage, particularly if the commodity involves iron, steel, sharp instruments, knives, cutlery, fire, and electronics. If you have business with any military department of the government, arranging contracts or collecting money, these will go smoothly.

Being so energetic, do take care during this period as accidents can happen – fire, explosions, burns, falls, blows. Slow down and be aware of what could occur. Sit down to eat instead of eating on the run, be aware of what choices you make, take your time and avoid indigestion, skin eruptions, or other blood disorders. With all the haste and rushing about, your blood pressure is likely to rise during this period so "make haste slowly!"

Fourth Cycle

Your mind will be very busy during these 52 days. It will be filled with new ideas that come so rapidly that you need to grasp them immediately; write them down before you lose them. You can rely on and act on your intuition, your hunches, impulses, make your plans now and express your thoughts. This is an excellent period for literary people, writers, journalists, book, and magazine publishers.

Now is the time to draw up new agreements, contracts, transfers, and other documents, but you must scrutinize any that are offered to you, as deception is in the wings along with tricky agreements and legal situations that are easily misunderstood. This is most definitely not the time to marry, buy a home, land, or a business. Wait until the next 52 day period.

Advertising campaigns, promoting your business to the public through newspaper and newspaper people, diplomats and negotiators have a much greater success now than at any other time in the year.

You will have to learn to pace yourself during this mentally restless time; finding yourself all tensed up won't do you much good, so break up your concentration on your work every hour or so. Go and talk with somebody, but nothing related to your work. Listen to some soothing music for 15 to 30 minutes or just take a quiet meditation time.

You will require more sleep and rest during this period, more than at any other time of the year, because your mind is going a mile-a-minute, pushing you to do more work than your body can really handle. When you feel yourself getting restless and uneasy, take a few days rest, get away for the weekend, and just relax. You will feel totally refreshed; then you can pick up the reins again.

Fifth Cycle

This is when your personal affairs have the chance for the greatest success. Money seems to come your way, your mind is clearer and sharper, business expands, relationships deepen.

You have so much confidence in yourself that you can begin any new ventures you have been considering even though they may take some time to grow. Large business negotiations can be planned now, especially if you have foreign countries or some international concerns in mind which can encourage you to take that long journey that you have had in mind for some time. Here you can mix business with pleasure.

Legal matters that have been pending can be dealt with successfully; lawyers, judges or the courts, government officials, prominent professional people, or wealthy people can be of assistance to you now in whatever business developments you have in mind. If you are owed money, ask for it. You can also speculate successfully in the stock market or in real estate. Make sure the transactions are absolutely legitimate.

Your health should be in excellent condition; if not, it will improve rapidly, especially if you will make time to spend outdoors in the fresh air. Nature is a great healer; absorb its energy and give your physical, mental, emotional, and spiritual bodies a great boost.

Sixth Cycle

This is the time for rest, relaxation, amusements; it's vacation, holiday time, making short trips here and there interspersed with renewing friendships which had lapsed during the busyness of the last two periods. New friends could well come on the scene introduced by other friends or relatives.

Business can still be attended to during this cycle, but at a more relaxed pace as executives and managers will also be taking their vacation time. However, if you are the owner or in a high position of a business that deals with art, artists' materials, beauty preparations, antique furniture, high-fashion clothes for women, oriental rugs or high-priced cars, stay with it, as this is the best period of the year for you. Your rest period can come later when business slacks off somewhat. Make sure you establish personal relationships with your customers to help your business along in the future. Now is the time to put the company's money into sound investments or to buy stocks and bonds, form partnerships or subsidiary corporations.

You will be tempted to overdo things during this cycle, eating, drinking, work or play, and having an exciting time all round. Remember these words when the next cycle comes along, as you may have to physically pay for your indulgence.

Seventh Cycle

This is the most critical of the 7, relating as it does to the number 9 cycle we discussed in the personal years. These 52 days cover the used-up, worn-out parts in your life that are no longer needed or useful for your further development. Let them go and make way for the new cycle and fresh starts that are waiting to begin. Some of you may feel a sense of loss that will tempt you to take foolish action or make stupid decisions to hang onto what you have. Impulsiveness or following your hunches will bring on disaster and you will look back later and wonder why you did this or that in your moment of fear or despondency. If you have any decisions that you feel you should make, hang on until the next cycle when things will be much clearer for you and your optimism is back in place. Older people can be of help and guidance to you right now with some of their knowledge and wisdom of the world. They can offer you emotional support and suggest practical and common sense answers that can be directly applied to your problems. This tenseness is a negative state of consciousness that prevents opportunities, interesting and exciting things entering your life that are just waiting to fill the void you have created by letting old areas of your life fade away. Relax back and let them in.

If you are in real estate or your job/career is involved with mines, minerals geological survey, archeology, or has to do with anything deep in the earth or in hidden places, this is a time of success. If you need to apply for patents or copyrights for inventions or writings, this is the time to do it.

Did you pay heed to the words of the sixth cycle regarding your health? If not, you are likely to be physically at a low ebb when you can easily pick up contagious germs. Steer clear of large groups of people and children (who always seem to carry germs around with them). Relax and find some sort of recreation that appeals to you, maybe something you have wanted to do for a long time and never found the time to get on with it. Your mind and spirits will go up and down during this cycle while bits of the "old you" drift away, making room for the new you. When you feel like this, think back on all the wonderful things you have accomplished during these previous cycles and personal years. Smile, remember the happy times you have had in your life and look forward to the next round of achievements and happiness and this cycle will soon be over.

As you read through these interpretations, you will recognize that the 52-day segments fit very nicely into your personal year. This adds further valuable information relating to physical, health, and business opportunities to the personal year, plus your challenges and rewards.

Chapter 12
Love and Compatibility

What brings two people together or keeps them apart? The energies that you share between you. What the two of you create. Your relationship as two independent entities, with separate personalities, each having your own secret fears and insecurities, your relationship with yourself and your relationship with your partner. This is quite a lot to think about when the two of you want to get together. Numerology has a lot of the answers, many of them you have already found within the chart you made of yourself. No doubt you have seen how one sided your view of reality is, and your tendency (like most people) to vent your problems and difficulties and guilt onto other people. Having learned a great deal about yourself through numerology you will recognize that relationship problems lie within ourselves through one-sided views and lack of self knowledge. After all, how can you expect to get along with somebody else when you don't even know who *you* are.

When you set out to take a journey of any kind, you need a road map first which you can buy at any gas station. But for this inner journey that you are taking you can't buy it, you have to draw your own map – numerology is one of these. As you have discovered so far, it gives you insights into your own behavior and motives, it is an archetype of the energies and drives that make you the person you are. The make up of your inner stuff, the emotions, drives, fantasies, dreams, desires, conflicts, loves, hates, and talents are elements that attract the same kind of elements to you from the world around you. So in effect, what *happens* to you is a reflection of something within yourself. Thereby hangs the tale of mutual attraction! If you are unaware of your inner self, you will continue to attract to yourself all sorts of things, people, and situations for good or ill. The more you know of yourself the more choices you consciously have, especially when choosing the right mate.

How are you going to make this choice? If you are just curious and not too serious about a relationship, you can get a brief report of the compatibility with a lover, friend, boss, family, or anybody else just by looking at the life path number of the person you have chosen, then comparing it with your own life path number.

If you have forgotten how to do a life path number you simply add together all the digits of the birth date of the person you have chosen so you will need to ask for it. When you have the number, look at your own life path number (from your own birth date) then consult the general interpretations below. For instance, if your life path is a 4 and your partner's life path is a 7 you would look for Combinations of Number 4, then find 4 with a 7.

These are just "quickies" so don't rely on them too much. We shall get into developing a more in depth relationship shortly by comparing Claudia and Cody's complete charts.

Combinations of Number 1

1 with a 1

A 1 with a 1 is rather a competitive combination, both wanting to be "top dog," each wanting to reach a greater pinnacle than the other. There is too much in common here for a good relationship of peace and harmony with both of you having the same ideals and ambitions. If you understand what the other wants out of life and can avoid being competitive, you *can* reach great heights together. As far as romance goes, there's not a great deal of love and trust here.

1 with a 2

Number 2 will rely on number 1, which is fine if number 1 is the caring type and needs a bond of affection and emotional security. Certainly there is coziness, but it can be boring, as there is little stimulation. In business, it works extremely well for the boss and his/her secretary.

1 with a 3

Here is a great sharing of imaginations. This is a long term, exciting, lively combination. You can do business together, each firing each other's creativity. You will enjoy the social rounds together and gathering of friendships and best of all you will share in each others love.

1 with a 4

These two are totally incompatible, so don't even try. You will usually battle over decisions to be made regarding a goal or a project. When it comes to love or business dealings, there is so much negative energy flying between you, the association is just not worth it. Suggestion: Each find someone else!

1 with a 5

A fine romance goes on here, lively, vibrant, full of passion, providing there is no codependency or jealousy. If this happens, the flames of love and desire will die a quick death.

1 with a 6

This is an excellent combination for two who are thinking of becoming business partners, as long as each of you don't insist on having everything your own way. Ideas should be suggested not forced. In this way you can create a great deal of money. There will be harmony in the home, if the 6 will understand and take it easy with the temperament of the 1.

1 with a 7

A somewhat difficult relationship in a marriage situation with 7s being quiet and introspective. If you can understand and accept the nature of a 7, you can enjoy a platonic relationship, especially if you have the same interests of culture, history, music, and crowd scenes only at certain times.

1 with an 8

This is a good match for both business and marriage. Two materialistic people who want to make as much money as possible and get as much out of life as they can. Dreams, ideals, and aspirations can be shared and talked over without each competing with the other.

1 with a 9

The number one will have to be the stimulating member of this association as the 9 can carry around a somewhat discouraging energy pattern. It's a tempestuous and emotional partnership frequently ending in heart break and scparation.

1 with an 11

This relationship is usually very successful. The 11, being the visionary, will add fuel to the number 1's ambitions. Any joint creative endeavor will be fruitful, so will both love and business.

1 with 22

I think you should both stay away from each other for these numbers represent ego and power struggles with the number 1 taking a beating. There is neither love, business, or friendship to be gained in even trying to combine these energy numbers.

Combinations of Number 2

2 with a 1

Number 1 of course, will be the dominating number to the submissive number 2, but you won't mind that. You will build a great deal of happiness in this relationship as you will be the inspiration in this cooperative endeavor.

2 with a 2

It seems like an ideal situation with both of you having the same views, likes, and dislikes. Happiness and friendship will last for a while until you both see that you are just extensions of each other; then an identity crisis will happen and that will be the end of a love relationship or a business partnership. Best not to get too close right from the start.

2 with a 3

Hard work again with this combination. A 3 can't be bothered with the ins and outs of 2's emotions and negativity, so fireworks and tempers erupt. If 2 will apply the social graces and charm and let 3 do the leading and creativity, then the association could last quite a long while.

2 with a 4

These two have a lot to offer each other in the way of strength and mutual aid, emotional and financial security. Home and domestic affairs appeal to both, but 2s could get rather fed up with 4's over-organized routines.

2 with a 5

Let the 5 do all the talking, appearing witty and clever, while you take a back seat until your strength of mind and moral support are required. This way, you can be sure of a friendship, a lover, and a successful business partnership.

2 with a 6

Love and a business partnership do well with the 2 and 6, providing money earnings, material success, forming corporate business organizations. Ideas and obligations will be shared; both of you are inclined towards some form of charitable work. Everything will be fine unless 2 decides to have a tantrum of jealousy or possessiveness. You each need room to breathe and grow.

2 with a 7

If you want to build a future together, each bolstering the morale of the other, then go ahead. Remember that 7 needs time alone for meditation and introspection. If you are both inclined towards mysticism, psychic research, numerology, astrology, and secret things, you will hit it off well. Starting a business venture together will also do well.

2 with an 8

This is the most loving and compatible combination of all the numbers. Together, you gain material success working out clever plans which boost your reputation and prestige. Socially you are looked upon as an exciting couple who enjoys a good time in the company of friends and with each other.

2 with a 9

You two can make a powerful combination if 2 puts practicality into the relationship while 9 puts in the imagination. Each of you can add strength and power to the personality of the other. If you don't understand what you both can offer in this relationship, then forget it and walk away from each other because you will never be happy within an icy bond.

2 with an 11

This a master number and all will be well between these two numbers as long as 2 does not try to eclipse the 11. A teacher-student or guru to chela is a far better combination than a love affair.

2 with a 22

Parent to child or an older person to a younger one is the combination that works best here. In business relationships, 2 should stay in the background being rather subservient, as 22, being the master number likes to be at the head of everything.

Combinations of Number 3

3 with a 1

Number 3's energy and vitality added to the leadership of the number 1 insures fame, fortune, and happiness for this duo. Concentrate together on a single project at a time, if you take on too many at once you are likely to blow the lot and experience losses.

3 with a 2

This combination works well if research and literary work is carried out together. A 3 has the talent and magnetism, while 2 can supply the practical application for 3's ideas. Balance must be maintained here for success.

3 with a 3

Like attracts like, each finding the other person highly attractive, both enjoying the social side of life. There is more of a childlike or young approach to life with these two. This is a friendship more than a lover or business partner. Grandparents with children is a great relationship.

3 with a 4

This combination is not recommended. There is too much friction between 3's imaginative and creative leanings and 4's down-to-earth approach. If you must get together, 3s would do well to listen to 4's practical advice, but there will be continual complaining about each other.

3 with a 5

The flames of passion and enthusiasm burn high between these two, but they are extinguished fairly quickly when interest runs out and someone else comes on the scene. There is usually not enough seriousness here for the two of you to build a family or a business together.

3 with a 6

Now here's a nice relationship. Building a family or a business together, the 6 will add the balance to 3's playfulness, making the relationship most congenial. If 6 decides to run everything on his/her terms, then 3's wandering eye might just upset the balance.

3 with a 7

These two numbers are usually incompatible, but they can actually stimulate each other if they will both take an interest in the talents of the other. The originality of the 3 combined with the inventiveness of the 7 could bring about very successful projects.

3 with an 8

The 8 will lead here with a most marvelous love affair which may or may not lead to marriage. If it does, then 3 will need to take a back seat and let 8 do the leading with its intellectual financial genius. A 3 can contribute bold ideas and creativeness which could work well in business.

3 with a 9

Both of you want to be the star of this show and if you want to get along you will need to learn to share the limelight, then it will be a good combination for both love and business. Father and son should stay at arms length and the same with mother and daughter; the energies are just not congenial.

3 with an 11

This combination makes better friends than lovers as 11 takes on the role of mentor. Together, these two numbers can succeed very well in an unusual creative business.

3 with a 22

There is no love relationship between these two numbers but they make fantastic business partners. 22 recognizes the tremendous creative ability of the 3 and invariably supplies the funding necessary to get the business on a successful footing.

Combinations of Number 4

4 with a 1

This relationship requires a solid foundation provided by the number 4, while the 1 provides originality and initiative. If 4 is irritated by the pushiness of 1, projects will not get off the ground and the relationship is likely to fall apart.

4 with a 2

The two of you can cooperate quite nicely if you both understand each other, each bringing out the best in the other. You can share emotional and financial security. If 2 gets bored and annoyed with your constant routine making, then it should be brought out into the open and discussed.

4 with a 3

Patience and tact is required in this relationship if it is to be long lasting. Your interests in research, medicine, herbology, mysticism, subjects that are unusual may not be of much interest to number 3. If that is the case, then the alliance will probably fall apart unless there are other factors in the two charts that will bring them together.

4 with a 4

This is a good match for both love and business as you share the same goals and values. The combining of these two forces brings financial success with philanthropic intentions when fortunes are made.

4 with a 5

Talkative and flighty, 5 needs your balance to successfully carry out any plans and ideas that 5 comes up with. Don't rely on the 5 or you will be disappointed as 5 always has too many irons in the fire with very few coming to fruition because they get abandoned on the way.

4 with a 6

This is domestic bliss with mutual trust. You can form a brilliant association together with 6, providing the originality and you bringing in the firm foundation for prominence and material gain. Without each other you would just remain plodders along the path of life.

4 with a 7

You plod along and 7 sits quietly interested in what is going on in his/her inside world with not much interest in the outside. There is not much of an energy exchange here unless you can take the results of 7's vivid imagination and produce a worthwhile outlet for it. (Like being an agent for 7's talent).

4 with an 8

These two are the empire builders of both money and large families – the families eventually producing many successful descendants. This a fun and profit-making relationship, both of you having an excellent sense of humor as you work hard to achieve your goals.

4 with a 9

With your practical application combined with the foresight of the 9, this could be a wonderful friendship. It is not very likely to be a successful love affair or long-term marriage.

4 with an 11

A 4 and an 11 should really stay away from each other, as 11 has nothing but contempt for 4's pedestrian and material outlook on life. An 11 has its head in the spiritual clouds and 4 has disdain for 11's lack of practicality.

4 with a 22

An excellent business relationship with you acting as the gopher and the hard worker. Probably a difficult love or marriage relationship, although both will be good parents.

Combinations of Number 5

5 with a 1

Two lively people who should get along very well with each other, a lovely romantic relationship. The originality from number 1 and speed from yourself will teach you both a lot about the other, including number 1 trying to rein in your busy tongue that never seems to take a break.

5 with a 2

This is either a "yes, we can make it together" or "we can't" situation. Certainly there is mutual respect, but, because number 2 is so quiet and self effacing, you can get thoroughly fed up with the martyr-like effect. That could be the end of this friendship or business partnership.

5 with a 3

You can do extremely well together for the forces of your energy patterns speak total success, whether it is money, corporate affairs, or organizational matters. Whatever you touch will do well because you complement each other.

5 with a 4

You will be attractive to the stolid number 4 person because you have a lot of the traits that they desire and need. If you add your quickness of thought and movement to the practicality of the 4, then 4 can supply the foundation that you need to bring your ideas and creativity to fruition. In time, you may be able to halt the nitpickyness of 4 to let a little light into life, work, and relationships.

5 with a 5

You are both rather mercurial by nature, so it is likely there will be periodical temperamental outbursts. You both have flighty, talkative tendencies, which you need to control if you want to get anything constructive out of this relationship; also understanding you each need to be free individuals with your own life styles.

5 with a 6

You will need to stimulate the number 6 person as they are quite home bodies in a lot of ways. You can bring out the intellectual powers and the initiative which is needed to cement this relationship. A great deal of compromise will be necessary although marriage and business endeavors will be a bit dicey.

5 with a 7

The best relationship with these two numbers is as friends as you will drive 7 to distraction with talk, talk, talk. You can certainly have a good time together if you can remember to rein in your verbosity; then you can actually fall in love or even get into business together.

5 with an 8

When you two fall in love, it's for a lifetime and beyond. An 8 has the steadying influence and practicality that the talkative 5 needs. Follow the example that 8 offers, develop the special bond between you; then great happiness will be in store for you both.

5 with a 9

This is not the best relationship because you may encourage 9 to gamble or take on risky ventures of any sort. There is a lot of wit and humor between you and you should listen to the vision and foresight of 9 to make this relationship work.

5 with an 11

Two free spirits who like to talk, you can spend hours exchanging the different adventures you have had. You will get on well together, but you are both as unrealistic as one another about money so you should not go into business together.

5 with a 22

This is purely a business relationship built on mutual respect with 22 at the head of things. You will supply the creativity and many of the ideas and 22 will see them through to a monetary conclusion.

Combinations of Number 6

6 with a 1

You two should be careful to give credit to each other's ideas and accomplishments, otherwise sparks will fly, especially if number 1 is trying to outdo you. Mutual projects can be very successful; it is excellent for a business partnership.

6 with a 2

You can provide the ideas in this combination, while the number 2 can work them out very successfully. The only problem here is that 2's jealous or obsessive streak may surface, spoiling a very compatible relationship.

6 with a 3

You two have much in common, although you will be the quiet one in this association. You can make long-lasting plans between you as this relationship is likely to last a very long time.

6 with a 4

With you both being serious types, you should be able to work out some very interesting plans between you that bring financial security backed by love and domestic bliss.

6 with a 5

This is quite a powerful relationship. Your experiences and what you have learned over the years added to the originality and quickness of mind of the number 5 makes a most interesting intellectual combination for success.

6 with a 6

There may not be enough friction between the two of you to make an exciting romantic relationship but you will give each other a lot of pleasure as your natures are very similar. You can have fun together as well as sharing your interests in serious mind developing subjects.

6 with a 7

Your interests differ widely here so there are likely to be clashes of temperament. If you want to make a go of this relationship, you would each have to learn to give in to the other to keep the peace. Is it really worth it when there are a lot of other people in the world?

6 with an 8

This can be an excellent relationship that has high possibilities in both business and romance but you will have to let the number 8 do the thinking and taking the lead while you put the break on any excessive or wild ideas.

6 with a 9

There seems to be some deep spiritual type connection here that is likely to last a lifetime once it gets going. There is friendship, partnership, collaboration, or marriage all tied up with mutual understanding and a depth of love.

6 with an 11

There is not much in common between these two numbers. Although 11 recognizes your love of beauty and art, it doesn't sit well with 11's idea of spiritual beauty. You would soon get tired of 11 spouting metaphysical thoughts.

6 with 22

Whenever you meet a 22, it means you have to take a backseat and let 22 be the boss. This is a working relationship that can last for a considerable time with your creative input.

Combinations of Number 7

7 with a 1

A platonic relationship built on friendship, likely to last a long time if the interests in history, culture, and social affairs are the same. You can put a break on the over enthusiasm of the number 1, adding your analyzing ability to bring in material profits. This would give pleasure to you both.

7 with 2

This is a placid relationship with little friction between the two of you, but not a great deal of excitement either. You will both have an interest in philosophy and occult subjects, so there will be great discussion times together and with friends.

7 with a 3

A lot of activity goes on in this relationship with the liveliness of the number 3. How long you can put up with the vibrant energy of the other person depends on your own endurance and acceptance, so don't be surprised if things fall apart.

7 with a 4

There is a strong combination here with you, the quiet one, supplying the ideas and number 4 will work them out with a firm foundation beneath them. In this way you will get along well together.

7 with a 5

Unless you have a streak of wildness in your makeup, number 5 will totally exasperate you. You will have to steer this relationship if you want it to continue. A 5 is all over the place, rushing here and there, rarely completing anything unless somebody has a firm thumb in their back most of the time. Do you really want your peace of mind disturbed to this extent?

7 with a 6

This is a very difficult relationship, demanding too much compromise from both persons. There is very little harmony and it will take too much hard work to make this relationship work.

7 with a 7

You two are somewhat similar, but you may be inclined to criticize each other and each other's work. If you can maintain mutual respect and recognize that you are equally intelligent, you may be able to make this combination work for quite a long time.

7 with an 8

Your vision and sensibility added to 8's executive and practical ability will ensure all the material requirements you both will enjoy. Give plenty of encouragement to 8's dreams and enjoy a happy life together.

7 with a 9

You two should get on well together as you both have a great understanding of universal laws. You both have compassion, understanding, and sympathy, which you are inclined to share with the rest of the world. In fact, it could be said that you two may be soulmates.

7 with an 11

You two are friends and lovers, but marriage will not last too long between you. There is not enough stamina. A business partnership would also fall apart eventually.

7 with a 22

You two are not destined to go or do anything between you. All that exists here is frustration with 22 being thoroughly annoyed with you not following instructions or going off into one of your introspective and meditative moments. This relationship is not recommended at all.

Combinations of Number 8

8 with a 1

Being powerful and aggressive types, you'll either get along well together or you will hate each other and become rivals. Together, you can combine your ambitions and go places or you can eventually annihilate each other. You have a choice.

8 with a 2

Being an 8 energy pattern and always being in charge, you will find the only thing this number 2 can give you is cooperation as far as business affairs are concerned. The other more valuable offering is the love that is given which will last a lifetime on which you will thrive.

8 with a 3

You both have the same aims and ideals which makes you an ideal pair. You both possess a magnetic personality and a strength of character which attracts others on a business scale. You can take 3's creative ideas and make a considerable amount of money from them by adding your practicality. The pair of you make great lovers.

8 with a 4

There is such a perfect understanding between you two, you don't even have to discuss your aims in life or even what you are seeking from each other. You should be the leader, of course, because you have just that much more power than the number 4. Romance, marriage, or business is perfect for the pair of you.

8 with a 5

If you want to get along with the number 5, you will have to put up with a lot of chatter, but it might be worthwhile listening to some of 5's ideas and creative thoughts. It's actually an interesting combination for love, romance, marriage, and building a family together.

8 with a 6

We have two love birds here, but don't over power your partner with the strength of your personality and magnetism – save that for your business colleagues. You will get quite a bit of inspiration from your partner which will benefit both of you.

8 with a 7

This can be a very successful business partnership, but not so hot for marriage or friendship as you cannot understand 7's seemingly cold, intellectual brilliance. Have you really tried to get deeply inside 7's thinking patterns? Deep down there is a great deal of warmth and tenderness that rarely shows on the surface.

8 with an 8

This can be a perfect marriage and a wonderful business partnership if you both present a united front to the world. Each of you have so much power that you can extinguish each other unless you share it.

8 with a 9

This can be a beautiful union if you put your energy into the relationship, especially if you can see your way clear to do some charitable or philanthropic work with your partner.

8 with an 11

This combination should be just good friends or doctor/patient or therapist/patient or 11 being a close advisor. A business relationship or anything closer will not work too well.

8 with a 22

You two can do many things together, especially as business partners. A marriage between you will be strong and long lasting.

Combinations of Number 9

9 with a 1

You can add inspiration to this partnership while the number 1 adds original ideas, even inventive genius. Let the number 1 take the lead. If you are one of the emotionally challenged individuals, look out for a tempestuous relationship that will not last too long.

9 with 2

You will certainly get cooperation from this partner. You have the foresight and vision, but only a relationship of serenity exists here. There is no spark to accomplish anything. If this is what you want, then this will be a life without arguments or friction.

9 with a 3

The keen intuitive mind of the number 3 should blend extremely well with your own intellect and powerful personality. Both of you would like to have the limelight, but with 3's tendency to look for a good time, thinking only of the present and not of the future, leaves you to do the guiding for you both.

9 with a 4

You will have to work hard to get this team going, as number 4 is likely to stultify the relationship with its constant practicality and negative approach to life. If you can persuade 4 to take on your imaginative ideas and mental creations to build a firm structure, you could do well between you.

9 with a 5

This enthusiastic adventurous number 5 person could liven up a relationship at any time. A 5's love of change may cause missing out on opportunities, so you will have to be the goal setter.

9 with a 6

This can be a lifetime relationship as there could be a deep spiritual connection here from long times past. You are both rather profound people enjoying the depths of different subjects. The pair of you will probably be involved in community projects gaining a lot of respect.

9 with a 7

An ideal relationship for these two numbers, whether it is for marriage, a business partnership, or a lifelong friendship. Heart, soul, and mind blend beautifully between you with mutual understanding.

9 with an 8

You will gain a great deal from this number 8 who will offer you the practicality you need. Share your imagination and occult powers with this partner; let 8 put the plans into execution and complete them.

9 with a 9

Both of you are foresighted, psychic, and very deep. Could this be destiny carving out a profound bond between you? Look much more deeply into your two charts to find further qualities and traits that bind you together.

9 with 11

These two numbers usually end up as teacher and student. A good relationship could be built in the area of group teaching of metaphysical studies.

9 with a 22

Again there is the teacher aspect to this combination, but more on the practical line of 22 trying to get you to share your genius and develop it into something of a material nature with benefits for both of you.

Having dealt with the "quickies," let us now get into the true depth of a compatibility chart comparing Cody and Claudia's charts. If you are really serious about the other person, this is what you will have to do to find a congenial relationship between the two of you. Don't let the "quickies" put you off if the reading is not a positive one. Look at the whole charts together; the reading may well override the "quickie."

First of all I need to make a chart for Cody just as I did for Claudia and as you did for yourself. This way I can see who Cody is, where he is going, who he is going to become; then I can compare their two charts for the rapport between them. (Note Figure 2, Cody's chart, in the Appendix.)

Look at the diagram and you will see that there are no missing numbers from the values of his whole name. There is a full house here, all nine numbers in his triangles are activated in some way, and he has no karmic debt numbers either. This is fairly unusual. So is the 33 and the 55 before they are reduced. This looks like we have a highly evolved soul here.

We already know the values and energy patterns of the name of the Montgomery clan who have been living and loving for generations. Cody's inner self felt he should live up to the name like his brothers and sisters, but he wasn't sure how to do it (number 2). Cody, being the youngest (an unexpected gift, number 6, his mother told him) was loved, coddled, and his big family gave plenty of advice on how to run his life, everybody having a different idea of what Cody should do or become (number 6).This left him mightily confused and indecisive. See the two Ys he has – one in his Christian name and the other at the end of the Montgomery name. Y is known for indecisiveness, having a fork at the top of the letter, but with the Montgomery clan, there would always be decisions to be made within the businesses they operated. Later, when Cody became a lawyer, he would constantly be in the same position of having to make choices – to use or not use the information or evidence he had, to make decisions one way or another (number 2). The number 2 contains the law of opposites – of duality – his decisions mean failure or success in his work. A positive attribute of his choice of career meant that Cody would finally be the one giving advice instead of having to receive it from his family.

You will notice there is a 3 and an 8 missing from the family name which had an impact on Cody in his youth, but they *are* in his Christian names. He was able to make up the use of these energies later when he took charge of himself, structured his thoughts (number 4 which is dominant in his chart) and his ideas (number 5), making his decision to become a lawyer. His innermost desire, the 0, his first vowel value, a number 6, was eventually to become a judge (number 7).The 0 fits him perfectly, its meaning being judgmental, which is what he would have to be in his chosen career. Although the interpretation suggests it being a negative attribute, in this sense it is applied as a positive –that's the duality of numbers.

With the whole name number being a 9, he is rather idealistic. In his youth, he had visions of saving the whole world and putting it to rights. He learned a great deal about the avarice, greed, meanness, and jealousies of human nature during his early years of lawyering, which gave him some heartbreak until he learned he couldn't change people – they had to change themselves. He had to learn to judge people correctly, recognizing their dark sides as well as their good sides. That's when the practical intellect of his number 4 took charge and he could see the world from a different point of view (number 9).

With the M at the beginning of the family name and his middle name, plus the number 10 addition of the Montgomery name, he has inherited integrity, patience, willpower, and his ancestors' high standards and morals. It is not surprising that his dream of becoming a judge finally came to pass. Later in life, he was honored and revered for his humanitarian understanding of human nature and his very fair decisions.

In the early years of establishing himself, he worked very hard (number 4). He didn't have too much awareness of his identity, resources, and talents (number 1), due to his family coddling and protecting him. The number 2 in his first triangle doesn't have much strength; there have always been family and friends surrounding him. Later, there would be partnerships in his profession, then his partnership/marriage with Claudia which filled the desire of the number 2 for both of them. Eventually, his resources and talents would blossom (numbers 1 and 9) through the sharing and exchange of love he and Claudia shared (number 2). He also has a U vowel missing from his Christian names, so when he is feeling uncertain, indecisive, or unbalanced, Claudia is there with her support (her strong number 1) during his "down" times. He can be quite broody and indecisive while mulling over a difficult case – this is when Claudia's understanding nature comes to the fore.

Being a lawyer, he takes on other people's problems (number 6). He is a team member (number 2), he developed self confidence (number 1), decision making (number 2), became organized and detailed (number 4) handling the most intricate details, even when they become frustrating. He will work on them until he finds a solution; in fact, he can be a little obsessive and intense – that's the downside of the number 4, but that is also an unconscious reaching out for perfection (numbers 7, 9, and the 10 of Montgomery). Sometimes he gets very annoyed at the shortcomings of his clients (number 7), yet he has compassion and understanding deep inside (number 9).

Cody developed his own personal and distinctive style (number 3), both as a lawyer and later as a judge. He is an outgoing, extroverted, warm personality when he is with friends. Clients are also impressed with his personality, his initiative, and action. With his number 4's dominance, he has developed a calm nature. He is sensible, ethical, good at managing the great deal of money he makes (number 8) as he builds the firm structure for his later years to fulfill his dream. He has also learned that he can confidently rely on his own impressions rather than heeding other people's impulsive advice.

He was also wise enough (number 7) to be able to learn to close down his work day (number 4), most of the time, to take up hobbies of some artistic expression to relax his strenuous days, and release the tensions and the nagging insecurities that linger as he asks himself, "Did I make the right decision?" Following his intuitive sense, Cody decided to try his hand at drawing and painting, which is where destiny led him to Claudia. He eventually gave that up as he wasn't talented in that direction, but he turned his hand to carpentry (the building number 4) as an outlet in which he excelled and enjoyed. He frequently joked that if he ever became disbarred, he had another job waiting for him as a carpenter!

So destiny brought the lovers together. Claudia's life path added up to a number 8. Recall her birth date is November 11, 1966; that's 11 + 11 + 22 = 44. 4 + 4 = an 8 life path for Claudia. Cody's birth date is December 24th 1961; that's 12 (December is the 12th month) + 24 + 17 = 53. 5+3 = 8. Cody's life path number is also an 8. An 8 is the number of fate – destiny, so the spiral of time brought the two souls together. These two souls, vibrating together as an 8 life path understand each other's material world, each helping the other to enjoy the careers they have chosen without jockeying for a "me first" position. The 9s, the 6s, and the 10/1s in both their charts intertwine in various ways bringing them together as souls who have met before. They do have a lot in common, and some common ground is essential, but it is the differences in a relationship that make them strong. There is certainly a difference in their careers, yet both are dealing with people at opposite ends of the scale. Claudia brings beauty, fantasy, and light into the homes of people (number 6), while Cody brings justice (number 7) into people's lives.

Cody's number 1 is quite weak when it comes to assessing himself; his ego is not as enhanced as hers, but the strength of Claudia's number 1s are a valuable asset to him, helping him to develop the self confidence he needed to make strides in his career, polish his speaking ability (number 3) facing the public and the judge in a courtroom when he decided to make changes in his life and become a criminal attorney. One of his best features now is his communicating ability with his clients. In the courtroom, he is recognized for building (number 4) his cases with ingenuity and facts. In exchange, he is a valuable asset to Claudia in helping her to have confidence in developing her artistic ability (numbers 3 and 5) and, most of all, bringing to life her need for self discipline (number 7) and to stop wasting time. When she established her business, he was at hand to give her legal advice, arrange her contracts, and anything else that needed a lawyer's attention.

Cody's number 2 is also not particularly strong, but it was sufficient to awaken Claudia's conscious feelings of needing to be loved and wanted. Their number 1s and 2s coming together in this fashion created (number 3), a love affair producing a marriage. Their triangles were coming together rather nicely with their give and take. They both have deep personal inner desires. When achievement happens to one of them they both celebrate for each other without any feelings of jealousy; it makes them feel that life is worthwhile.

Claudia built her structures (number 4) with his aid and insistence on discipline (number 7). She has no energy/strength in her number 7 and learnt her lessons the hard way, until Cody took her in hand. He, on the other hand, had all the numbers in his chart, some strong, some weak; all it needed was Claudia's understanding of the depth of his feelings as he dealt with the tide of humanity's appalling existence. This also gave her the insight into why her father gave of himself to so many causes and organizations as his energy pattern of the humanitarian number 9 is the same as Cody's whole name number. Both, in their own ways have a deep spiritual feeling for humanity.

Both of their careers do well, on an even footing. Neither have the greed to make vast amounts of money at anybody else's expense. There is only 1 energy pattern in both their number 8 triangles. They are both aware that the talents they possess in the hidden recesses of their number 9s will be activated, regenerated, and transformed through their number 8s, balanced by their soul energies of the love they share between them and give caring and sharing to others through their number 6. They are very family oriented, not only with close family members but they draw other people into their orbits by making them feel loved and wanted. Claudia is an asset to Cody in his business and social world because people are naturally attracted to her. Having gotten over the aggressiveness and jealousies of her youth, she did indeed blossom into the beautiful flower giving love and beauty to others that Cody recognized was deep inside her. People are attracted to the spiritual light she carries around with her due to the love that Cody gives to her that has no words to describe. He, in turn, has his own loving energy pattern which makes people feel that they are the only ones who matter to him when they are in his company.

They have an ideal relationship of loving, caring and sharing, two souls existing as one. Of course they have their spats now and again with Claudia wanting to expand her business without giving it proper thought or making the necessary plans and financial decisions – her lack of number 7 again which crops up periodically. He, on the other hand, annoys her considerably when his number 4 takes over and he becomes a workaholic ending up feeling cynical and jaded over the case he is working on. She has to come to the rescue again and again, insisting on taking him away somewhere and pumping life back into him.

Now that they are both into their maturity stage, Cody having realized his ambition of a judgeship and Claudia being very satisfied with her business and the employees who manage it for her, life is at a more gentle pace. Both are happy and delighted over the accomplishments of their children. They have time together now to share their experiences, what lessons they learned from them and from each other, the outlook on life they have both reached, and to discuss the people they have now become.

May they have many more years and pleasures together as they continue to walk their life path together.

Chapter 13
Career Planning and Selection

Most of us have tried a number of jobs during our lives. I know I have, and when I got into numerology in the 1970s, I was very surprised to find that I had unknowingly tried quite a few jobs that the numbers suggested that fitted into my life path, but I continued to try this and that until I finally came to the conclusion that the numbers were right. What I really wanted to do was to write and to paint, but could I do it, did I have this hidden talent? I was afraid to give it a try. I harbored this desire for a long time (until I was nearly 40) when it dawned on me that my missing vowels (my deep desires) were saying the same thing. Eventually, I got up my courage and followed my path.

Years later, analyzing my own reaction to this information I realized that a lot of other people also missed out on their hidden potential because of their fear of failure. Nobody likes to make a fool of themselves.

Of course there are some people who start in on a job, perhaps their father got them into it, or it is a family affair and 30 years later they are still there. I wonder if they are really satisfied or contented with what they are doing. Perhaps the job has just become an acceptable habit pattern that brings in the money.

Then there are the handful of people who hit the bulls eye right from the start and they say, "I love my job; it's exactly what I want to do."

How about you? Are you happy with your life, with what you have chosen to do with your working days? If not, are you are just considering a change and can't decide what you want to do next; numerology has many choices for you to peruse before making your decision. You may find that it offers you employment potential that has never crossed your mind; on the other hand, what you read may give you the courage to follow your dream.

To investigate what the numbers have to offer, you will need to have your life path number ready. This is what you worked out in chapter 7.

For the benefit of the people who have turned immediately to this chapter for help and advice, you will need to calculate your life path number first, the answer being a number between 1 and 9, except for the power numbers of 10, 11, and 22. If your birth date adds up to one of these then you should read chapter 7 before continuing. To get your life path number you add together the month, day, and year of your birth. For instance, if you were born on March 1, 1976, you would add this all together. March being the 3rd month of the year you would add 3 + 1 + 1976 = 27 then 2 + 7 = 9. Number 9 would be your life path and you would consult the information below for the varieties of choices for number 9.

What would you like to do with your life? Now you can make your choice that is in harmony with your numbers, your personality and your character from your name numbers along with your life path number. Some people like to use their brain, some their brawn, others their creativity in a number of different ways. Some wish to serve by flying passengers from one place to another, as a waiter/waitress who serves up a hot breakfast to long distance truck drivers, or as the assistant who finds the right flattering evening gown for the rich lady who lives in the mansion across the park. There are leaders who know where they are going, followers who prefer a less stressful life. There are politicians, money makers, counselors, military folk, those who bring us relaxation through their entertaining. Caterers, beauticians, florists, teachers, healers, homemakers, fishermen, historians, professors, care givers, child minders, paleontologists, astronomers, astrophysicists, archeologists, scientists. Where do you fit in? Your career is in the numbers. Look at all the numbers you have found in your chart, consult the information below, mix and match and you should be able to come up with some wonderful ideas about where you should direct your career. Let's see what the numbers have in store for you.

Career Path Number 1

These are known as the leaders, the entrepreneurs, because of their independence and management abilities. You work best alone, where you make the decisions. Your own business, perhaps as a retail store owner or wholesale trader may appeal to you. How about the construction industry, engineer, inventor, explorer (James Cook, explorer, was a number 1 life path) technology research, the military, government institutions, ambassador, stage and film industry, program planner or director for film, TV, radio, journalist, fashion designer, athlete: swimming/running. The only thing that could spoil or inhibit your career is your impatience or being too bossy.

Career Path Number 2

Here are the diplomats and peacemakers; as a general rule they don't mind somebody else being in charge. You are very cooperative team players, often drawn to social or government work. Some of you will fancy the medical field of nursing, even into massage, acupuncture, physical therapy, counseling. Number 2s are often architects, musicians, music teachers, foreign diplomats, librarians, clerks, insurance adjusters, even negotiators for police, lawyers, or insurance companies, perhaps even becoming a lawyer in the field of labor relations or public relations. At the other end of the scale you are very good in the field of fashion, also as a jeweler/watch repairer, caterer (especially in the area of event planning). If you are wondering why there is such a variety, all numbers have a multitude of choices at different levels for different people due to the various numbers that are involved in your name and your birth date. Like life itself, numerology is based on recurring patterns and cycles and the energy within the numbers will impose themselves on you at various times to which your emotions will respond. These are the times when you are likely to change your career or lifestyle to something completely and totally different, surprising yourself, friends, and family when your life becomes precisely what you have always longed for.

Career Path Number 3

People with this birth path are multitalented. Graphic artists, cartographers, printers, actors, musicians, writers, film makers, speech writers, entertainers, public speakers, and teachers of elocution. You need to be in the expressive arts someway or another. Telecommunications, internet worker, journalist, newspaper/distribution, travel agent, tourism, interior decorator, landscape designer. You could be a model, a cosmetician, a nurse, dietician, a physician, child psychologist, or even a lawyer. Another option is becoming an athlete or athletic coach.

With such wide choices you will need discipline and commitment to achieve any one or more. One thing you must avoid for your own happiness is working alone or in isolation. This will break your spirit and creativity.

Career Path Number 4

You are the dependable, practical, reliable people with a keen mind for details. You prefer an organized environment so you would do well in banking, accounting, insurance, financial expert, investment counselor, as a government employee in a civic capacity, political science, or even into politics if you are ambitious in that area. The legal field may also appeal to you.

Other areas which may interest you are the armed forces, police force, construction, carpenter, mason, agriculture, mines, mechanic, engineer, chemist or lab technician, computer programming, enumerator, research, or as a professional boxer.

You may also consider managing or owning a restaurant, a retirement home, hotel, revenue property, catering service, or even becoming a numerologist, or an astrologer.

You should avoid any area that involves risk taking such as the stock market or anything that sounds like a "get-rich" scheme.

Career Path Number 5

People with this career path number often look to the sales field first as being their choice of career. You're an ideas person, one who needs freedom and movement. Apart from a variety of sales, think about public relations, a career in the travel industry, marketing/promotion, advertising, import/export, a talk show host or radio newscaster, TV, the entertainment field, the internet, film making. You have extremely good verbal skills as a master of ceremonies, a teacher of voice. Some of you will have strong language skills which could be used as an interpreter or language teacher, a diplomat or even an undercover agent, investigator, or detective. Two other fields 5s are often interested in are photography and botany provided they can be on the move in these careers.

Further choices are researcher, architect, explorer, artist, designer, publisher, writer, playwright, editor, and proof reader. For the less ambitious, consider a chauffeur, driver, driving instructor, and waiter/waitress.

Career Path Number 6

This number is concerned with home, their own and other people's requirements, so you make excellent realtors. Interior decorator, cook, caterer, home economics, event planning (a multibillion operation now); these last two could start as a home-based business and grow into something bigger.

For some, being a hostess or the hospitality industry will beckon, a foster home or being a foster parent, manager of an apartment complex, involvement in an animal shelter, or becoming a vet.

Music appeals to you. You could be a musician, performer, pianist, piano teacher, or teacher of other instruments. Other areas that could be of interest are fashion design, dressmaking, beautician, florist, writer, marriage counselor, divorce attorney or in the healing profession as a nurse, doctor, or herbalist. Some give their service as policemen or firemen.

Career Path Number 7

An interesting selection for the quiet number 7s ranging from counselors, personal trainers, medical professionals, cosmetic surgeons, dentists, therapists, researcher or research assistant/secretary. Being a lawyer, photographer, astrologer, psychologist, archeologist, undertaker, investigator of and writer of the unknown and occult side of life has attraction, so has the religious side in becoming a preacher or religious leader. There is a great desire for philosophy and a yearning for truth and education.

Other interests for the 7s include police work – CIA, CID or homicide, insurance fraud, analyst, scientist, criminologist, or as a veterinarian.

Career Path Number 8

This is very much a business and financial vibration. You are likely to be thinking in terms of banking, investor/investment counselor, being president, manager, or executive of a large company with ideas in the future of your own company. Government work, civic affairs, politics, congressman, professor of political science, business law, social work, and real estate are also of interest.

History appeals, especially in the area of scientific archeology. So does crime investigation, pharmacology, engineering, sports, journalism, publishing, and editing. You may fancy a literary career, perhaps you should consider "How To" books.

Career Path Number 9

The humanitarian number 9 also has a vast array of choices for a career including environmentalist and child protection services. Politician, lawyer, judge, narcotics agent, scientist, doctor, surgeon, professor, spiritual healer, teacher, researcher, and foreign correspondent.

At the other end of the scale is the interior decorator, photographer, horticulturist, landscaper, artist, or journalist, Some may be drawn towards the clergy exploring the spiritual side of life. Surprisingly, the number 9 can be quite a successful entertainer as a stage magician.

Career Path Number 11

Here are the artists, inventors, religious leaders, the inspirational teachers and lecturers. Writers, astronomers, astrologers, numerologists, graphologists, prophets, all fit into the 11 category.

The younger 11s will be caught up in the glamour of space flight, engineering and electronics and being an astronaut.

This number is one where success comes with maturity starting around the age of 35 to 45. Sometimes the 11s are still part of the number 2 (11 added together = 2). See the number 2 vocations also where that career path may appeal.

Career Path Number 22

This career path is very similar to the number 4 and the number 8 but on a much stronger scale and higher vibration.

It deals with large institutions, business, politics at a much higher level. School superintendents and librarians come into this category along with management and book keeping. Pilots and aircraft fit into this career slot.

Read up on the 4 and 8 vocations in case those career paths may appeal to you.

Just like ourselves, jobs and careers have personalities and energy patterns of their own. There are thousands of different types of jobs out there today and many more being invented by such creative minds who are tuned into the moving energies of the universe. Don't just stick with what I have written. I have tried to cover a multitude of choices, but if something from another number impresses you, give it a try. It may well be one of the other numbers that you have in your name or your birth data has pushed its influence into your emotional path.

With such a diversification of numbers you have multiple energies to work with bringing you quite a lot of different types of experiences throughout your life at different periods. When life offers opportunities and changes, go with it – you may well end up with a very satisfying adventure that you've never dreamed of.

Chapter 14

Your Home and Telephone Number

Are you comfortable with the energy patterns in the house or apartment you live in? Are you and your business address suited to one another?

If you are hunting for a suitable residence or business accommodation, the way to go is through analyzing the numbers attached to the building in much the same way as you analyzed your name for your personality and character.

All buildings give off an energy pattern; so do apartments, offices, and rooms within that building. Each has a number attached to it and this is its personality. But is it right for you?

When you are looking for somewhere to live or to start your business, take into account the numbers attached to the building. These will indicate the things or circumstances you will encounter during your stay there. The numbers can tell you in advance of the experiences or events you are likely to run into.

Before you make your decision, consider what you are actually looking for. What is your choice, your desire? Is it peace, relaxation, retirement away from the hustle and bustle? Or a place where all your friends can trundle in and out at all times of the day or evening? Perhaps you are looking for a home to start or raise a family?

All the numbers from 1 to 9 have something to say about the address you are investigating and if you are not completely happy with the one you are living in, they will shed some light onto the reasons for your discomfort which you may be able to alter.

To find the root number of the address you do it the same way you learned at the beginning of the book, adding up all the numbers and reducing them to a single digit. There are a few exceptions.

You do not use *st, th,* or *nd,* such as in 21st or 25th or 92nd, nor the words *street, road, avenue, suite, apartment, unit* – just ignore those. For instance, if the address is 311 Main Street, ignore the word street, reduce the word Main to its root: 4 + 1 + 9 + 5 (19) then add the 311 (5) the total is 24, reduced to a 6. The name of the street will indicate the surrounding neighborhood, the people, and the atmosphere around the place. The whole total is a number 6. In this case, a number 6; the area revolves around mothers who are at home or work at home so that they are there when the family comes home from school or work. It's a family oriented neighborhood and as the word Main reduces to 19 = 1 + 9 = finally a 1, the neighborhood will be cared for and looked after by the men who will tend to dominate the area. The beginning number 3 of the house suggests the men will get together, talk, talk, talk, asserting themselves (the number 1) in community affairs. In fact, the whole family will be quite social and creative.

If the avenue, street, or road has a name like Oak, Pine, Crawford, Hatton, or whatever, use these, reduce them to numbers, add the number of the house to get the full total then look at the number of the name to see what the neighborhood is like. As mentioned, do not use street, avenue, etc.

Just one more thing to remember. Some street signs point to North, South, East or West. Sometimes written in full, otherwise just the abbreviation of N, S, E, or W.

If the direction on the sign is written in full, reduce the full word. Let's say Broadway Avenue North. Ignore the avenue. Reduce the word Broadway – 2, 9, 6, 1, 4, 5, 1 ,7 = 35 = 8. North, written in full is 5, 6, 9, 2, 8, = 30 = 3. Broadway and North combined = 8 + 3 = 11 = 1 + 1 = 2.

Now, if the word North is abbreviated on the sign to just an N, which it usually is, then go with the abbreviation. It does make a difference. You'll note that Broadway is an 8, but now the N on its own is a 5. 8 + 5 = 13 = 4 so the overall environment of Broadway N is a 4, suggesting it is an older location, probably a number of character houses there where many of the residents have grown up. They know each other, likely went to school together. Home life is good all round and the houses have naturally appreciated in value since they were first built. It is a safe area, although it will have quite a lot of heavy traffic as the word Broadway suggests.

The number 2 root of the words Broadway North written in full is suggestive of younger people with all the up to date amenities of life, bought on credit cards – sound systems, TVs and telephones in each room, exuberant children, noisy fights now and again as the occupants are quite stubborn. Despite the fact that their gardens are well cared for, full of flowers and beauty, the inside of the house is usually in a state of disorder. You see what a difference the numbers can make.

For the folks who live outside the city, having no actual street address, use your legal description instead including any letters. Example: Lot 3, Block 26, Plan E4566. Add together 3 + 2 + 6 + 5 (the E) + 4 + 5 + 6 + 6 = 37. Reduce the 37 to 10 and the final number is a 1 property.

Property Numbers

We have 9 basic meanings which represent the final reduced number of the property you have in mind – remember they must be between 1 and 9. Here are the meanings of each house number.

Property Number 1

You will certainly feel motivated within the surrounding energy of this house. It's a property for an individual who likes to assert him/herself, taking the lead, setting trends.

A number 1 house attracts ambitious people, frequently career singles who enjoy living alone. Females, having to do any renovations or upkeep themselves, find their masculine side strongly developing. That's really not surprising when you find you have to mow the lawn, clear out the weeds, clean out the gutters and down pipes, change the light bulbs, mend the light switch, do the snow clearing. And whatever else needs doing. These are new experiences you will learn.

This number 1 house will constantly need repairs, but you have probably been attracted to it because its energy pattern makes you feel alive and vigorous. It's quite possible that you were at the point in your life when you needed a new start and destiny set your feet on this path.

Number 1 houses do not appreciate in value like the number 4. You will always be putting money into it.

Because of number 1's inner instinctive attitude towards getting rid of the old and making new starts, it tends to physically attract fire. Be careful with candles, open flames, make sure your fire and smoke alarms are kept in good working condition.

It's a vibrant house so enjoy it as long as you stay single. If you decide to marry, start looking for another. Two independent, assertive, impulsive people won't be happy under this roof.

Property Number 2

Peace, harmony, relaxation, and balance exist most of the time within the walls of the number 2 house. This is the house for the newlywed lovers. If you haven't actually tied the knot, getting married in the garden of this house would bring out the subtle energies of nature giving the two of you togetherness and happiness right from the start.

This house has a cozy, loving energy pattern to it, encouraging all kinds of relationships. Art, music, sensitivity, awareness, and intuition exist here, where deep sensual moments will be shared. The negative side of this love affair is that the pair of you will have to watch out for a pattern of laziness that one or both of you have. This will cause quarrels and fights, neither giving in, for you are both as stubborn as each other. Arguments often revolve around who is going to do the fixing, repairs, or the garden clean up with neither one wanting to take on the responsibility. Food is another attraction in a number 2 house, so watch your intake for you will most certainly put on weight.

Nevertheless, plants and paintings find their way into this blissful house; beautiful interior decorating adds to its sense of warmth and welcome. It's a good house that will appreciate well.

With number 2's double standard (1 + 1) this house is an excellent choice for a home-based business such as a beauty salon, tax services, or maybe buying and selling of gem stones. If you are looking for a business property in the retail market, look for a number 2.

Another interesting feature of a number 2 house that is really peaceful is that it attracts psychics and spiritually inclined people. This gives them the opportunity to carry out readings or teachings within the house and the business will do extremely well.

Property Number 3

This number 3 house is one that almost speaks from the walls itself. There are so many people in and out, there is constant communication, much entertainment goes on and many dinner parties and creative entertainment arranged. One thing that needs to be watched here is finances. With all the entertainment and parties, money outlay could be in excess of income, producing a blind eye towards responsibilities, the attitude being enjoy now and pay later.

It is likely to be a large house where journalists, writers, photographers, newspaper people, and other creative types gather to share their ideas. Restless people gravitate towards the energy of a number 3, often taking on a townhome.

Foreign correspondents who have to leave at a moment's notice and traveling sales people have a fondness for this type of home. Students are also drawn towards them. They band together to rent, study, and share. Artists, musicians, and authors feel the pull towards the mental energy that the number 3 exudes.

In fact, this is an excellent number for an art studio as it seems to encourage the creative processes.

Property Number 4

The number 4, the foundation and solidity of home life gives feelings of security as if being enfolded in loving arms. This is a property where people have stayed for a long time, perhaps generations and it has been passed on down through the family. It is usually well cared for and its market value is always high.

People who live in a 4 house spend much time in the kitchen. This seems to be the meeting place for family, friends and neighbors. The room is frequently large, plenty of room to gather there to eat or just talk. There's always good wholesome home cooked food available, much coming from a well tended garden.

Talk is often about the past and the golden moments of childhood and growing up. The thought of eventual retirement is generally in the background.

In fact, if you can obtain a number 4 house with retirement in mind you will experience a great deal of peace and contentment. Study the foundation and structure of the building before buying. This is often a problem of a number 4 house as many of them are character houses or have quite a few years behind them.

If you are looking for a revenue house, try for a number 4. When you have selected your tenants they will stay forever.

Property Number 5

The number 5 house, similar to the number 3 represents change, movement, travel, "let's go away for the weekend" type of people. Young people, noisy folk as a rule, lots of books and all the latest gadgets available that they will have to tote along when they decide to move – which is quite frequently. People who are impressed with the number 5 never stay long anywhere. They seek challenges and new experiences that keep them pepped up.

Being mentally and physically always on the move, they experience very little peace and relaxation. Bad tempers and arguments frequently erupt and the breaking up of friendships and relationships follow suit. There is a lack of stability, discipline, and responsibility all around with people who are inclined towards number 5. They are unconventional people, just like the houses, townhomes, or apartments they are attracted to. More than likely, they are involved in unconventional, unusual businesses where no two days are alike.

Property Number 6

Warm, caring, protective number 6. If you are family oriented, you will undoubtedly be drawn towards this number, this type of property. The natural vibration of 6 is beauty, love, nurturing, and compassion.

This is an excellent house for raising children because it offers a family relationship energy pattern. You will find the children are inclined to bring all their friends home with them. They too have the same warm loving natures and it wouldn't occur to them to ask first; they say, "Come home with me and meet my mom." Better have lots of cookies and milk ready – then you'll have to clean up again when they are gone, as this house is usually spotless.

Somebody in the household will be a gardener and it could be that the garden itself was the clincher that made you put an offer on the property. Inside, the house will be beautified to your own special color schemes and enhanced by the flowers from your own garden.

This is a house that encourages the neighbors to "drop in" unexpectedly. You'll have to put up boundaries right from the start of your occupancy or you will have little time for yourself. They will encroach on your privacy. Your house will make an impression on your children's friends; they will tell their parents who just have to see it. Gossip abounds in neighborhoods and soon everybody will want to have a peek. Beauty attracts. When you make something beautiful of your house and garden, it stimulates all five senses. People cannot resist so be prepared.

Property Number 7

This can be an interesting house if both people are on the same or similar path in life or they really understand each other.

If you are looking for a peaceful retreat to relax from the pressures of thc world, a number 7 is for you. It will also open your spiritual sense, leading you into private and personal introspection.

Is your personality/personal expression (name number) a number 7? Then you are a naturally reserved wisdom seeker who enjoys the quiet, the silence, and exploring the spiritual realm.

A lover of water and water's energy, your garden will probably have a pond, pool, or fountain. Inside you will likely have fountains of different sizes in various rooms, small table ones, maybe a floor model, too. An interesting feature of the word water is that if you add together the consonants of the word, they add up to a 7. That's the W, the T and the R = 5 + 2 + 9 = 16 = 7. Water is a vibrant part of the number 7 so keep your awareness open occasionally for defects in your plumbing system.

Another side of the 7: If one partner is the quiet type, highly mystical and in tune with the emotional self and the other one is exuberant, always on the go and not really interested in spiritual things, this challenging relationship will not last too long. Number 7 can bring the breaking of contracts, divorce, litigation but on the other hand, if an understanding can be brought about, the alive energy of one partner is excellent for the quiet number 7 to be drawn into the outer world at times, thereby balancing the inner world. This opens up opportunities for a wonderful relationship and the sharing of a fascinating number 7 house that increases in value.

Property Number 8

Number 8 is the wealth builder. It is a most auspicious number. It represents the infinity symbol if it is turned on its side. Infinity contains everything. Within it is the opportunity for wealth, health, happiness, advancement in the material world if organization, discipline, and vision is employed.

Much business goes on within these walls. It's a powerful house. Executives, lawyers, politicians, and doctors are attracted to the energy of the 8. It offers success, financial abundance – and money goes out just as quickly as it comes in.

The morals of the number 8 should be strictly adhered to as they will be brought into play here as these walls are imbued with both the light and the dark energies of those who have lived in it. The hidden forces of the universe will show their natures. You could make a fortune in investments for instance, but if you are using other people or their money for your own selfish means, then the universe will see that you eventually lose big time. The same applies if you are a politician and serve only yourself.

With the number 8, honesty is absolutely essential along with a high moral standard. This number, more than any others deals with karmic debts and karmic lessons.

Young couples starting out together can build their own empire if there is a strong, deep love between them. As long as they understand the morals of the universe and the temptations of underhand power plays that will be offered them, their love and material wealth will gradually grow as will the value of their property.

Property Number 9

If you take on a number 9 property, don't expect it to increase much in value. You are not very likely to make a great deal of money living here. You will occasionally receive the unexpected windfall, but the atmosphere itself is calm and mostly productive. It's more the home for the intellectual – writers, professors, scholars. It's also a place where groups frequently get together to discuss foreign affairs.

There is probably a considerable library here, a busy fax machine, a lot of internet activity and paper work taking place with people in different parts of the world. Through this a broader picture of humanity takes place, intuitive patterns develop leading into an understanding and acceptance of the different traditions of society throughout the world. At this time a philosophical view of life takes place.

Medical people, social workers, and the visionaries of this world are drawn towards a number 9 property. Quite a few become involved with organizations that offer them world travel working with under developed countries.

Non intellectual people usually stay a long time in a number 9. They are patient, compassionate folk, raising a family, seeking security and stability. They establish a career, eventually reaching their goals or a pinnacle of achievement plus their spiritual and personal growth.

When it comes to renting or buying an apartment or business premises the same principles apply. There are of course, two numbers to work with, one of the apartment or suite of offices and the other for the street number.

Add the numbers of the apartment or the office, then separately add up the street number. The apartment or office number will give you the atmosphere within which you live or work. The street number will give you the general atmosphere of the area.

If you combine the totals of the apartment or office number with the street number you can get a pretty good idea of the experiences you are likely to have while you live or work there. When you have added up your numbers and reduced the digits to between 1 and 9, consult the previous information for the houses.

Your Telephone Number

Your telephone number will have a similar impact on your sensitivity and personality in the same manner as your name, birth date, and house number have an effect on you. It's your response to the energy pattern within the numbers and the atmosphere they continually generate which bring experiences to you.

Add up the last four digits of your phone number right now and see if it fits your life style. Does it bring you the communication you want? If it doesn't, then change it. Phone companies usually allow you to choose a number from a list they will offer you.

Let's say you are in business for yourself in the wholesale textile industry. You find it slow, the phone doesn't ring as often as you would like, it is not generating enough business and you have to extend yourself to make the sales and break even.

Counting the four digits of your phone number you find it comes to a 7. This is not a good number for business, especially sales. You need a 3 or a 5. The remedy? Change your number as soon as you can, inform your clients of the change, advertise your new number, and see the difference it will make in the future.

When you are analyzing your phone number you need only to add the last four digits. This is the only portion of the number that personally applies to you, your family, or your business.

The area code of your number applies only to the energy pattern of the whole province, state, or area it covers. The prefix gives you an idea of the general atmosphere of the people who inhabit that area. The remaining four digits affect you and how you will respond to them.

Telephone Number 1

This is an excellent number for business and career. It generates a great deal of personal power with which you can influence others. Being a masculine strong number, it tends to be a bit short on awareness and sensitivity, but if you can recognize and handle this fault, then your business will do well. If you have children in your family it would be advisable to get them their own phone.

Telephone Number 2

This is a sensitive diplomatic number. Singles will constantly be on the phone to each other with lovey-dovey conversation. If you have a service-oriented business, this number suggests tact and cooperation if you want your business to grow, but if you are a strongly opinionated person, others will not cooperate with you and you will lose opportunities.

Telephone Number 3

This number indicates a busy phone, whether it generates business or not is another matter as the number itself lacks focus and direction. There are lots of ideas and motivation attached to the 3 energy. Young people will share them, but unless there are goal-oriented and ambitious people among the group of chatterers, nothing much will come of them.

Telephone Number 4

This is a number that really belongs to companies like banks, accountants, or law firms. It is a good, solid dependable number giving out dependability and trust. If you work at home in a one-person capacity, this is an excellent number. It is also a good choice for large families who wish to keep in contact with each other.

Telephone Number 5

All sales people should have a number 5 telephone; so should people who are constantly on the move. Unconventional people are always drawn towards a number 5. The phone is constantly in use, frequently making very successful sales pitches, despite the lack of discipline and responsibility. There is a tendency to forget to phone their families.

Telephone Number 6

This is the family phone always in touch with each other. You will need more than one phone in the house as everybody likes to join in the conversation. When the phone eventually becomes free, the children will grab it to talk with their friends. The number 6 encourages gossip!

Telephone Number 7

This is not a number for business; it suits scholarly people, educationalists, deep thinkers, researchers, and spiritually minded folk.

Telephone Number 8

This is a good business number attracting money if you are ambitious and motivated. Career and finances will grow in leaps and bounds. It's a practical, materialistic number, not suited for anyone who is seeking spiritual growth.

Telephone Number 9

If you are looking for material wealth, forget the number 9. With its idealism and compassion, this number is suitable for non profit organizations, pro-bono lawyers, health clinics, and those who wish to help the unfortunates of this world. Occasionally, these organizations receive unexpected money from people who are inspired by the work that is being done or they will benefit through donations and wills.

Conclusion

So we come to the end of the book, but not the end of your search for yourself. This is a neverending lifelong journey. Every time you have new 1-9 cycles, other aspects of yourself reveal themselves within the challenges and rewards you will experience. They are always different. No cycle is ever repeated exactly because life is handing you another set of adventures.

You could consider a 1-9 cycle as the chapters of a book, and each further 1-9 cycle as the sequels. Think of all the jeopardy you have been through already in your previous years and how your next move then decided which way the game of life took you. Was it the excitement of a new beginning, happiness, joy? Or was it sorrow, heartbreak, loss? Whatever is waiting in the wings for you, even if you think you have been through it before, you will experience it on a totally different level, from another viewpoint because your previous experience brought a transformation of self – inner, outer, mental, physical, emotional, and spiritual.

Provided for you in the Appendix is a blank Numbers of Your Life chart for you to begin to chart your own life. If you can read your numbers as they are written, your life long journey will be one of continual fascination. You may not always like what you discover but it will eventually lead you down a path of unexpected bliss.

Appendix

Alphabet with Corresponding Numbers

Letters	Equal	Number
A, J, S	=	1
B, K, T	=	2
C, L, U	=	3
D, M, V	=	4
E, N, W	=	5
F, O, X	=	6
G, P, Y	=	7
H, Q, Z	=	8
I, R	=	9

Easy Chart to Copy and Place on Your Wall

1	2	3	4	5	6	7	8	9
A	B	C	D	E	F	G	H	I
J	K	L	M	N	O	P	Q	R
S	T	U	V	W	X	Y	Z	

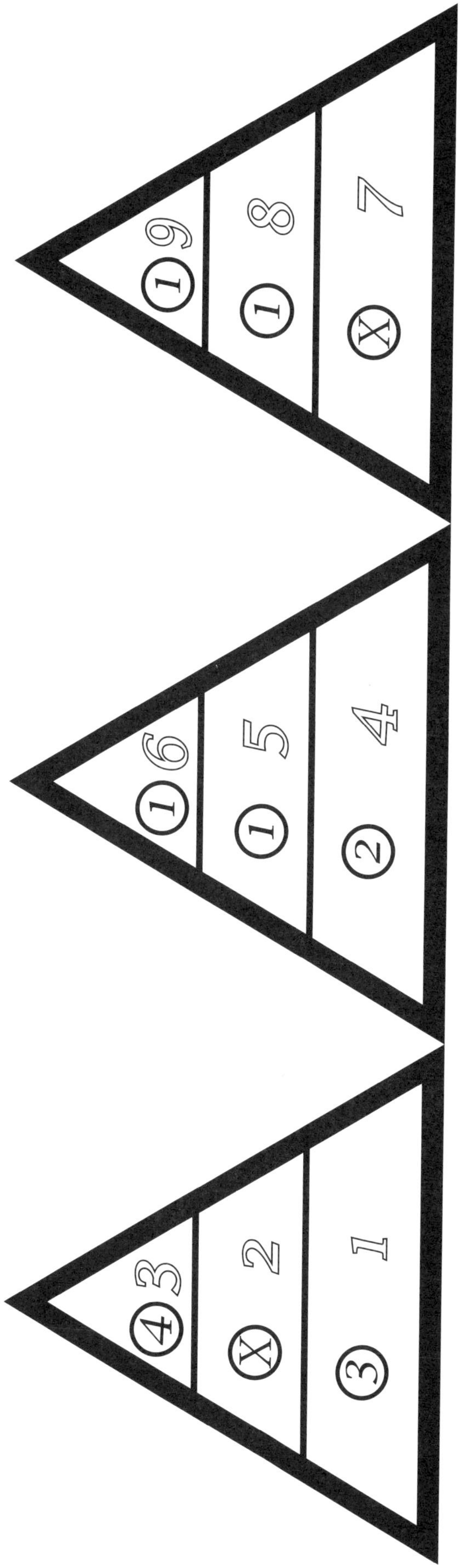

Figure 1

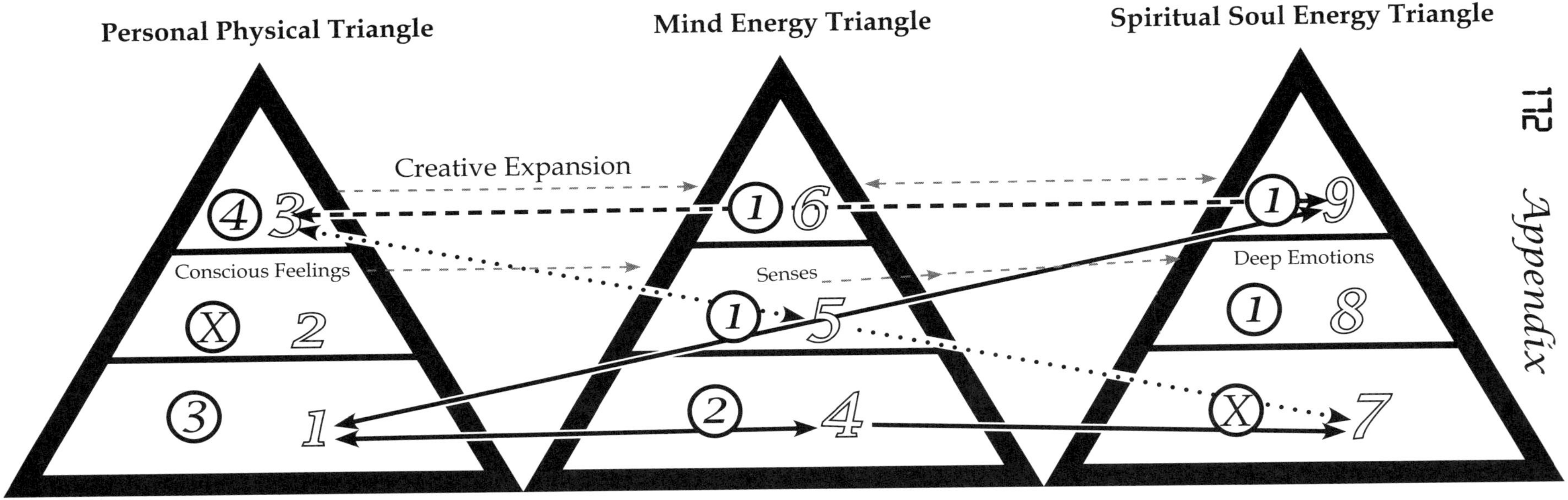

Material World 1---- 4 ---- 7

Number Value From Whole Name

1	=	3
2	=	–
3	=	4
4	=	2
5	=	1
6	=	1
7	=	–
8	=	1
9	=	1

14/5			1	3		9	1			6			5		= 11/2
	C	L	A	U	D	I	A		H	O	L	M	E	S	
	3	3	1	3	4	9	1		8	6	3	4	5	1	

= 24 = **6**   = 27 = **9**

Whole Name = **6** + **9** = 15 = 6
Claudia's whole name vibration is a number 6.

Vowel Value = 14/5 Karmic Debt
Consonant Value = 10/1 Strengths
First Vowel Value = A = 1 Strengths
First Letter Value = C = 3 Strengths
Balance Number = C + H = 3 + 8 = 11 = 2

From Christian Name
Missing Numbers: 2, 5, 7, 8 - Weak Links
Missing Vowels: E Deep Desire
Missing Numbers from full birth name: 2, 7
Birth date: November 11, 1966
Life Path Number = 8
Challenge Numbers: 0, 2, 2, 2
Reward Numbers: 22, 6, 1, 6

Figure 1A : Claudia's Chart

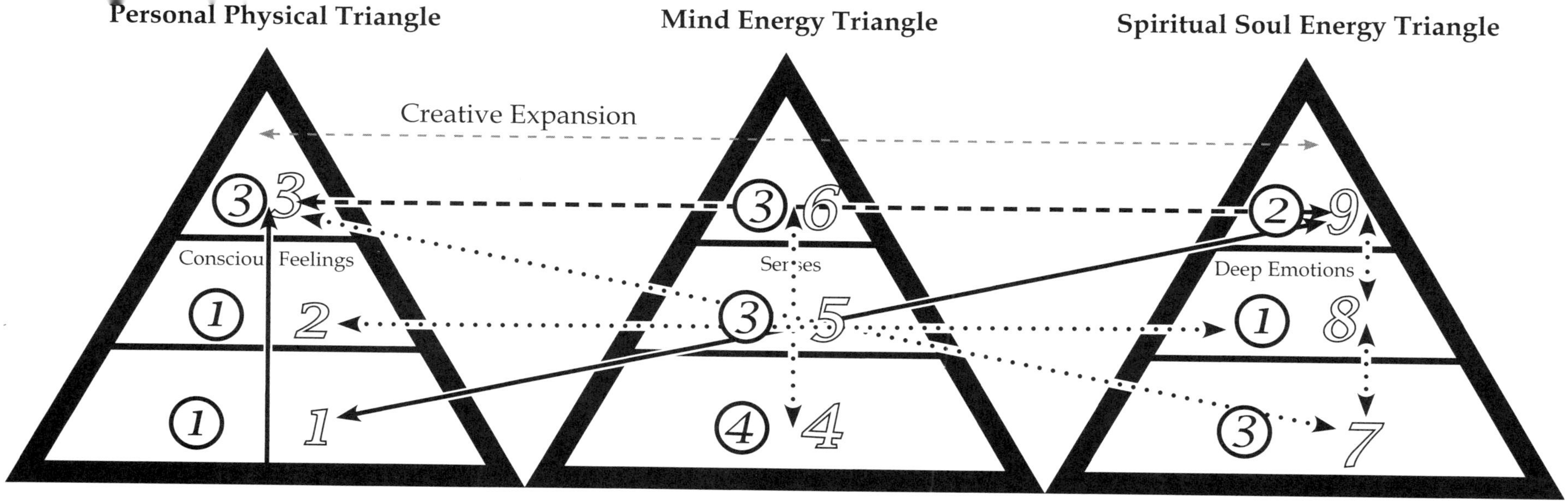

Material World 1---- 4 ---- 7

Number Value From Whole Name

1	=	1
2	=	1
3	=	3
4	=	4
5	=	3
6	=	3
7	=	3
8	=	1
9	=	2

	6			= 6		9			1	5		= 15/6		6				6		5			= 17/8	Vowel Values
C	O	D	Y		M	I	C	H	A	E	L		M	O	N	T	G	O	M	E	R	Y		
3	6	4	7		4	9	3	8	1	5	3		4	6	5	2	7	6	4	5	9	7		

= 20 = **2**   = 33 = **6**   = 55 = 10 = **1**

Whole Name = **2** + **6** + **1** = 9
Cody's whole name vibration is a number 9.

Vowel Value = 6 + 6 = 12 = 3 Karmic Debt
Consonant Value = 14 + 18 =32 = 5 Strengths
First Vowel Value = O = 6 Strengths
First Letter Value = C = 3 Strengths
Balance Number = C + M + M = 11 = 2
3 4 4

From Christian Name
Missing Numbers: -None- Weak Links
Missing Vowels: U Deep Desire
Missing Numbers from full birth name: None
Birth date: December 24, 1961
Life Path Number = 8
Challenge Numbers: 3, 7, 4, 4
Reward Numbers: 9, 5, 2, 2

Figure 2 : Cody's Chart

7 Cycles

Cycle	Date
First:	
Second:	
Third:	
Fourth:	
Fifth:	
Sixth:	
Seventh:	

Personal Physical Triangle — Mind Energy Triangle — Spiritual Soul Energy Triangle

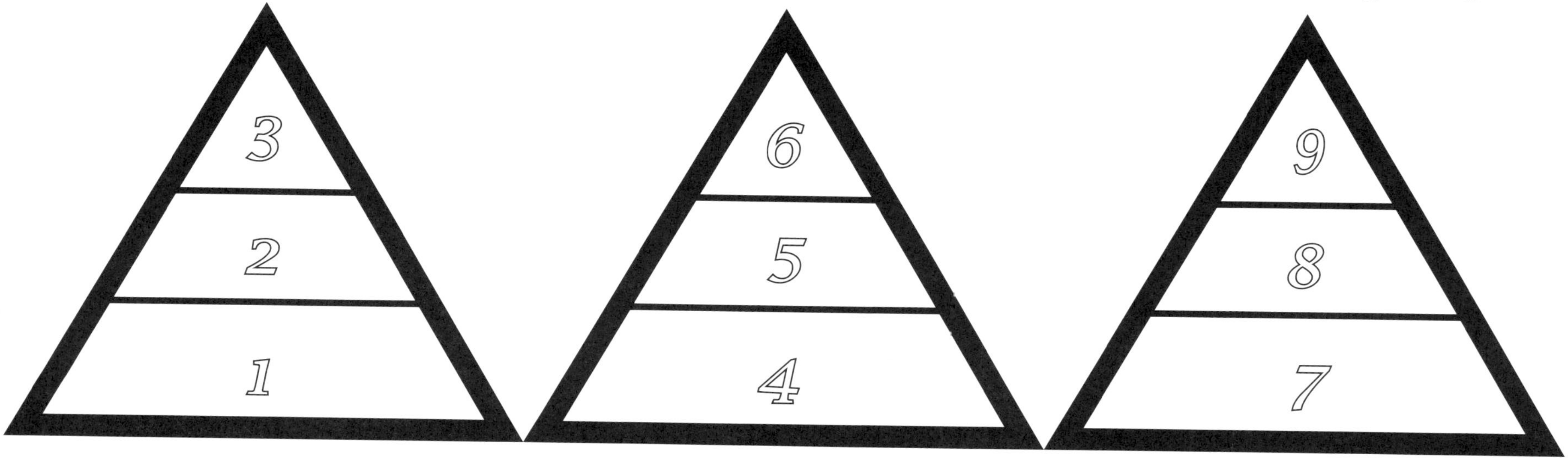

Material World 1---- 4 ---- 7

Number Value From Whole Name

1	=	
2	=	
3	=	
4	=	
5	=	
6	=	
7	=	
8	=	
9	=	

Vowel Value = Karmic Debt
Consonant Value = Strengths
First Vowel Value = Strengths
First Letter Value = Strengths
Balance Number =

Name =

Whole Name =

From Christian Name
Missing Numbers: Weak Links
Missing Vowels: Deep Desire
Missing Numbers from full birth name:
Birth date:
Life Path Number =
Challenge Numbers:
Reward Numbers:

Bibliography

Decoz, Hans. *Numerology.* Berkeley Publishing Group, New York, NY. 1994

Goodman, Morris. *Modern Numerology.* Fleet Press Corporation, New York, NY. 1945

Gray-Cobb, Geof. Numerology Workshop. 1979

Gray-Cobb, Maiya. *Angels The Guardians of Your Destiny.* Ozark Mountain Publishing. Huntsville, Arkansas. 2008

Gray-Cobb, Maiya. *Seeds of the Soul.* Ozark Mountain Publishing. Huntsville, Arkansas. 2009

Nomenology Project. *The Hidden truth of Your Name.* Randon House, Inc. NewYork, NY. 1999

Shine, Norman. *Numerology.* Simon & Schuster, Inc. New York, NY. 1995

Teacher Lesson Plans and Resources

Medicine Wheel Education
Approved by Karen Whetung

9 781989 122938

Table of Contents